FOUND DOGS

ELISE LUFKIN

photographs by
DIANA WALKER

HOWELL BOOK HOUSE
New York

Howell Book House

A Simon & Schuster Macmillan Company
1633 Broadway
New York, NY 10019

MACMILLAN is a registered trademark of Macmillan, Inc.

Library of Congress Cataloging-in-Publication Data available upon request from the Library of Congress.

ISBN: 0-87605-597-8

Manufactured in the United States of America

10 9 8 7 6 5 4 3 2 1

Book Design by George J. McKeon

This book is dedicated to the matchmakers: the people who work to place homeless animals, professionals at shelters as well as individuals with their networks of friends and neighbors.

CONTENTS

ACKNOWLEDGMENTS

I am grateful to Ariel Cannon at Howell Book House for her belief in this project and for her help in making it a reality. Other people as well have given me encouragement and significant help in different ways. I would like to thank Colleen Daly, Jim Agnew, Bash Dibra, Susan Duncan, Peggy Howell, Sue Lavoie, Bob Langendoen, Peter Mayle, Linda and Russell Munson, Michele Stephenson, Bunny Williams, my daughters, Elise, Margaret, Alison and Abigail, and, of course, my partner in crime, Diana Walker. Finally, for the stories in this book as well as those precluded by lack of space, I would like to thank all the generous people who were willing to tell me about their rescued dogs. This book really belongs to them.

Author's Note: All profits from this book will be donated to animal-related organizations: several animal shelters, the American Humane Education Society and the Delta Society.

IN PRAISE OF LOST AND FOUND DOGS

Even after spending what seems like a lifetime with a dog who claimed to have been abandoned, I am still not sure about who found whom. It certainly wasn't a conscious decision on our part, nor were there any of the usual formalities—no exploratory meetings, no test walks, no quiet moments alone together to assess mutual compatibility. It was all very sudden. One day, there he was—threadbare, thin as a bone, exotically perfumed, and clearly with no pressing attachments or appointments. We were told that he'd been interviewing passersby in our local village in France for two weeks before he caught sight of my wife and decided that she might be suitable. He accompanied her home. That was ten years ago.

He has since been joined by another refugee, a ruffian who made eyes at my wife from the back of a pickup truck. It turned out that he, too, was open to offers, having finally exhausted the patience of his previous owner because of his unorthodox diet. (This included computer cables and one or two other items we needn't go into here.) He came home as well, and so we found ourselves with two canine orphans.

Neither one is a shining example of the purity of bloodline that causes breeders to sigh with pleasure as they mentally tot up the stud fees. The senior dog, Boy, can be taken—when the light is right and the critical faculties have been temporarily suspended—for a rough-haired French pointer, steady under fire and swift on the pounce. But appearances are deceptive. Years of closer acquaintance have shown him to be more interested in lunch and tennis balls than in hunting.

The antecedents of Alfie, the other dog, are even more murky: part Irish wolfhound and part Airedale terrier, or so the story goes. My own view is that his mother was swept off her feet by a lurcher with a particularly seductive set of whiskers. The result of their union is interesting and unusual, some might even say bizarre. It's safe to assume that Alfie will never be troubled by the inconvenient celebrity that accompanies Best of Breed.

Never mind. What these two charming bastards lack in respectable pedigrees they make up for in other ways, and I'm sure it's the same with most dogs who get a second bite out of life. A found dog never takes anyone or anything for granted. Somewhere in the deep recesses of the orphan psyche, never entirely forgotten even after years of good living and kindly, obedient owners, memories of harder times linger. And this, it seems to me, tends to give lost and found dogs a special appreciation of what the world can offer. They have more *joie de vivre* than dogs with a settled, traditional upbringing. They take an extra delight in the small but rewarding joys of daily existence—the digging, the rolling, the ritual burial ceremonies, the unauthorized chewing of precious objects, the fine unselfish distribution of mud and undergrowth. It's as though they realize that fate has granted them an extension, and they are determined to make every waking second count.

This enthusiasm naturally extends to their owners in a number of ways. You can expect fierce loyalty, extravagant displays of welcome after even the briefest absence, adoring glances, unsolicited gifts (sometimes small and long dead, but it's the thought that counts)—no effort is spared to make the human part of the household feel secure and wanted. And it doesn't take orphan dogs long to embrace the idea of sharing: your bed, your furniture, that lonely and neglected leg of lamb you left in the kitchen, the new cashmere scarf, a favorite book. There is no trace of snobbery or discrimination. If it belongs to you, they're prepared to give it a try, such is their eagerness to fit in with their new surroundings.

Within a matter of weeks, they will have adjusted. They will have marked out and claimed their territory, and decided on their friends and enemies. And here, it's often possible to see mysterious formative influences from their pasts at work. One of our dogs, for example, is threatened by the approach of anyone wearing a hat. The other is relaxed about hats, but considers the UPS man a burglar in disguise. What might have happened to cause these phobias we shall never know, but they have the effect of transforming two normally affable animals into banshees that would give the Hound of the Baskervilles a run for his money. In my more evil moments, I wish they could be persuaded into being equally unwelcoming to any visitors with bills, magazine subscription opportunities, or invitations to cocktail parties, but I think they're too good-natured.

In fact, these noisy aversions to men wearing hats or bearing packages are the only traces of antisocial behavior that we have seen in either dog. Whatever indignities or hardships they might have had to endure in previous lives have been put behind them. All dogs are forgiving, as we know, perhaps none more so than the stray who has landed on his feet.

Another, more practical advantage of orphans is that they are survivors, with constitutions toughened by early circumstances. They aren't reared on creamed chicken and warm beds, shielded from draughts, protected from distemper, hardpad, colic, infant gripes and all the other ills of puppyhood. They live rough in those youthful days, and it pays off in later life. It makes them much less prone to ailments than the delicate creature with the yard-long pedigree. They require less cosseting—as happy with an old blanket on the floor as a down-filled throne—and they tend to have the digestive capabilities of a waste disposal unit. During his first week with us, Alfie's gastronomic experiments led him to consume a chicken carcass, a rattan wastepaper basket, a car seat belt, an entire cushion, the skeleton of a giant horseshoe crab and a small, rather handsome fruitwood box with contrasting inlay. These were in addition to his routine rations, and one can imagine the catastrophic effect this would have had on a sensitive, aristocratic stomach. But Alfie thrived on it, with never a hiccup.

One last thing that appeals to me about the stray with muddled ancestry is that wherever he might have come from, it wasn't a mold. Much as I admire and like certain breeds—Labradors, let's say—one of them tends to look very much like the next. It's the same with Irish wolfhounds, Dalmatians, basset hounds and dozens of other great canine families: the specifications are consistent, and that leads to a certain uniformity. You know what you're getting, both in appearance and behavior.

But when you adopt a dog, the whole experience is fraught with delightful unpredictability. Very little is certain—except, of course, that you will be giving him a better life. And he will be doing the same for you.

PETER MAYLE

xi

INTRODUCTION

I can't remember a time in my life without a dog. The Christmas card my parents sent the year I was born is a photograph of a plump, smiling baby trying to pull herself up on a very patient, large, white dog. When I was ten, a small terrier mix turned up at our house one day and captivated six children in about five minutes. She then set out to charm my parents, a more difficult challenge which took the better part of a day. Sweetie Pie stayed with us for fifteen years. Dogs shared the exuberance and fun of my childhood and comforted me through bouts of painful shyness. Fortunately, there was always a dog for solace.

Diana Walker, photographer and creator of the moving and evocative images in this book, has also shared her life with dogs and understands well their capacity to enhance our existence. Diana's life has always included dogs; one of her earliest memories is of the family's Norwich terrier, Strawberry, giving birth to a litter of puppies in the basement. Diana is quick to point out that her love for dogs has in no way smothered, or even affected, her passion for cats, nearly fifty years of cats—Abdul, Daisy, and now, Fred and Ginger.

My dogs have made happy times happier and difficult times bearable. This bond has enriched my life immeasurably. A minute ago, taking a break from my desk, I realized that I had a dog's head under each hand and my foot resting on a third—bliss for all four of us! Working at an animal shelter and participating in a pet visiting program at a nearby nursing home have increased my interest in the relationship between people and dogs. Dogs can give us so much pleasure; they comfort us, make us laugh, even lower our blood pressure when we stroke them. In the same way, a person can provide a dog with a good home, attention and love; one actually has the power to give a happy life. Unfortunately, people also can be ignorant, irresponsible, and totally lacking in compassion. Our animal shelters are full of unwanted puppies born because owners refused to spay and neuter their dogs; young dogs who were cute as puppies but, untrained and neglected, became unruly nuisances; dogs abandoned when owners moved; and old dogs brought in because they were too much trouble—dogs discarded like Kleenex.

Happily, there are also people willing to open their hearts and homes by adopting some of these abandoned animals. *Found Dogs* is a collection of portraits of such people with their adopted dogs, some from animal shelters, some picked up on the street, a few who just followed someone home. In it, you'll find the stories of people who, in reaching out to a needy animal, have enriched their own lives. The relationship between a person and his or her dog can be a very special one, particularly in our society, where loneliness is a serious factor for so many. Owners have told me again and again that their adopted dogs seem to appreciate the opportunity they've been given and are especially loving. Of course, not every dog in an animal shelter will be the dog of one's dreams.

That depends on making a good match at the outset and a real effort on the part of both dog and owner to fit into one another's lives. Training a dog so that it is a pleasure to be with him, and then including that dog in one's life as much as possible, can lead to great happiness for both dog and human. Whatever we give to a dog will be repaid over and over, with interest.

Perhaps these stories about generous people who have reached out to needy dogs will inspire others to do the same. However, it is not always an easy road and should never be taken simply out of pity. A dog, and particularly a second-hand dog, is a big responsibility. Regular meals, regular exercise, training, health care, and lots of time and patience are basic requirements. Still, the satisfactions are enormous and the need is great.

I hope many more people will consider sharing their lives with an unwanted animal. Our shelters are full of dogs just waiting, many in vain, to be given a chance. Last year, more than three million homeless dogs and puppies were destroyed in this country alone.

Doing the research for this book has been a joy, and during the past three years I have heard many great stories. I only wish that space allowed all of them to be included. One of my favorites was told by Peggy, a volunteer for FOCAS (Friends of County Animal Shelters) in San Diego.

PEGGY'S STORY

Recently an older man came to the pound. He explained that he wanted to look for a dog that had been born after March 20, and I commented that he must want a puppy. He replied, "This is a rather unusual situation. Do you believe in angels?"

"Of course," I answered.

"Well, do you believe in reincarnation?"

I assured him that I could believe in almost anything if it would help him to adopt a dog. He then explained that on March 20 his beloved little dog of seventeen years had died. He was devastated. Then one night an angel had appeared in a dream and announced that his dog would return but that he would have to look for her.

"So here I am to start looking," he said.

Together we walked through the shelter going from floor to floor, passing cages filled with all kinds of dogs. Finally in the last aisle back in a corner he spotted a dog. He looked at the dog. She looked back at him, and he said, "There she is!"

I pointed out that this dog was definitely not a puppy. She was three or four years old and quite large as well. Nevertheless, I opened the cage, he held out his arms and the dog rushed to him. "I'll take this one, this one is mine," he said.

The dog followed us to the office where the man filled out some forms and paid the adoption fee. Then I opened the door leading to the parking lot. The dog then led the man out the door and walked directly over to his car where she waited by the passenger door for him to come and open it for her. They both got in, and off they drove together.

FOUND DOGS

DORSEY

SUE LAVOIE

Dog trainer

While I was working at an animal shelter, I agreed to take a wild, one-year-old white German shepherd to housebreak him and to try to make him more adoptable. Dorsey went home with me to my husband, Bob, and our four dogs. Dorsey had never been in a house before, so for two or three weeks he paced and panted continually. He was very head-shy; if I reached out to pat him, he would duck away, and if I moved quickly, he would run out of the room. One day I picked up a rake and he yelped, ran to the far end of the yard and cowered in the corner. He was so nervous he made *me* nervous, and I could hardly wait for someone to adopt him.

Gradually, after several long months, he began to settle down. Then one day a man came to the shelter to talk about adopting him. I did the screening myself. The prospective owner seemed okay; but when I went home, I felt terrible. I looked at Dorsey, and I thought, What if you do something wrong, and they yell at you? What if they hit you? You'll go right back to the nervous wreck you were. I went outside to the picnic table and began to cry. After a while, Bob came out.

"Why are you crying? I should think you would be happy to get rid of him."

"But he trusts us," I said, blubbering.

"Well," said Bob, "I always told you we should keep him."

So we adopted Dorsey—six years ago. Now he acts as a demonstration dog for the obedience classes we teach. He has a Companion Dog title in American Kennel Club obedience competition. He is a qualified Search and Rescue dog who has participated in searches all over the state, and a weekly visitor at the local nursing home where he charms everyone with his calm, friendly ways. Some residents save cookies for him, and one blind woman likes to trace the shape of his head and ears with her hand while she talks to him.

Sometimes, at home, when he sits near me, puts his head on my knee and looks at me with those big, brown eyes, I remember that wild, frightened young dog.

EL SOL

JON KELLAR
Construction worker

One day while I was doing some volunteer construction work at our local shelter, I saw the shelter manager, Alison, and the vet carrying a dead dog out to the incinerator. It made me stop and think. Some of my friends had been saying I should get a dog, but I wasn't sure. I talked to the people at the shelter and to the vet about what is involved in owning a dog, the costs of food and medical care, exercise, all the ins and outs of dog care and—in my case—an increase in the rent.

After he went over medical expenses—the regular ones, such as yearly shots, and the unexpected ones, such as injuries—the vet added, "If you decide to get a dog, you should be prepared to spend at least one hour of quality time with him every day." That is some of the best advice I've ever had.

When you're thinking of getting a dog, it's important to know what you're getting into. I would recommend talking to the people at the shelter, talking to a vet, and reading a good book on adoption like *Second-Hand Dog,* by Carol Lea Benjamin. It helped me think about what I hoped to find in a dog and what having a dog would mean in my life, for better and for worse.

After doing all this research, I called Alison at the shelter and told her I was interested in getting a dog, an active adult dog who could go with me when I was biking or cross-country skiing; I wanted a dog who didn't bark, probably a golden retriever. I was willing to wait, and I did wait for three months until one day Alison called to say, "I think we have a dog for you." Later that day I ran into Loren, who works at the shelter, and she said, "I think we have a dog for you." When I went home, there was a message from my friend Ginger. "I think they have a dog for you at the shelter."

Boy, did they have a dog for me, a beautiful golden retriever: El Sol. He was two and a half, really sweet, knew how to sit on command, never chewed; he was outstanding.

I decided to start right out with exercise for our quality time together. After work, I bike or cross-country ski, depending on the season, and Sol runs. On weekends we go exploring in the mountains. Every day we do something, even if it's minus 20 degrees outside. It's just a habit I've developed, and it's paid off big time.

I'm pretty sure that's why I've got such a great dog. He comes when I call—that's key. He's usually ahead of me, so when I say, "Sol," he makes a big U-turn back to me and waits until it's okay to go on. He's with me constantly; I take him to work, and he hangs out by my pickup. For the first year or so I tied him up near the truck so he couldn't get hurt; now he stays around without being on a leash. Of course, he doesn't get much attention at work, but he likes to know where I am.

Sol's a companion, a pal; I really appreciate the simple pleasures he provides, like sleeping next to the bed at night and being there to say good morning. He helped me get to know my neighbors. I had been here several years and didn't really know any of them; Sol knew them all the first week, and now I do too. People say it's only a dog, but that's not the way I feel. A dog takes a lot of work and a lot of money, but it is so well worth it in the end. Any time that guy has a smile on his face, it puts a smile on mine.

FLASH

PATTI LOUSEN (BOWMAN)
Mom

JULIA BOWMAN

CLAIRE BOWMAN

Patti: My husband and I wanted to get a young dog, but not a puppy. We wanted a calm dog, a good companion for the girls, not too rough. We went to the animal shelter to walk dogs, and I liked Flash right away. He was certainly not young, but he was good-looking, quiet and easy to be with. His owner had died, and her husband brought her dog to the shelter the next day. Just imagine how the poor thing must have felt! We took him home, but it was difficult at first. He must have missed his owner, because he certainly was depressed for months, all through the winter. By spring he seemed to get over it. He's happy to see us now when we come home, and he has a bounce in his step, even though he is quite an old dog.

Julia: When Mom or Dad can't hold me, I go to Flash. He's nice and cozy. I like him because he's old.

Claire: I want to keep Flash forever.

BEAR

GERRY CURRIE
Truck driver

A few years ago I had just two dogs, older dogs. I knew that when one died, the other would be lonely, so I went down to the shelter. There was Carbon, a young Lab/collie with his tail wagging, looking at me as if to say, "Please. . . ." As soon as he moved in, he started running the older dogs ragged, so I had to get him a playmate. That's Cheyenne, a German shepherd/Australian shepherd mix. She was a year old, and so nervous for the first four or five days that she hid under my truck in the garage and only sneaked out to eat and drink at night. She soon got over that, and now she rules the roost. Then there's Runt, a Newfie/Pyrenees I couldn't resist at the shelter. And, of course, Bear. . . .

A friend who knew I liked Newfoundlands heard about a woman who was looking for a home for a male Newfie about a year old; my friend talked me into going to see him. The owner made a big deal about how she hated to give the dog up, but when I saw Bear and the situation, I said, "Let's get him out of here!" It was winter, very cold. He was kept outside without even a real doghouse, just an open lean-to. His food was a frozen block; he had no water bowl but drank from a little muddy ditch. His fur was filthy, matted and full of burrs. He had to climb up ice-covered steps to a deck with sliding glass doors just to lie there and look at the people inside. I am not a violent man, but I wanted to smack Bear's owner for the way she treated that poor dog.

We did get him out of there with no mishaps. It took a few months for him to get used to me and the other dogs (and to being in a house), but now I can't walk from one room to another without Bear following right beside me.

He's not the only one. All the dogs want to be next to me. Every one of them was neglected before; now I guess they're making up for it. When I take a shower, they pile into the bedroom; and if I didn't close the door, they would be in the bathroom and probably right in the shower with me. If I have a glass of milk, everybody wants a taste. When I lie down on the sofa, Bear—a 140-pound fur rug—wants to lie on top of me.

People say I'm crazy. Maybe five dogs is a bit much, but when I come home tired and aggravated, they make me feel better. I admit I spoil them, but I'm happy and they're happy. Who could ask for more than that?

THELMA

LENI MAY

Dog lover/bridge player

PETER MAY

Businessman

Leni: As a kid, I grew up with dogs, but Peter never had a dog and was even a little uncomfortable with them, so for years we had none.

Peter: I thought a dog would be a major lifestyle pain in the neck.

Leni: Then I turned fifty, stopped smoking and went crazy. One day I passed a pet shop, and I thought, That's it, I'm getting a dog! I asked a veterinarian friend to help me find one; she just happened to have a stray, a shepherd mix with the unlikely name of Princess. When I went to see the dog, she wobbled down the stairs, half-starved and nearly hairless with mange. She also had a severe case of heartworm. I took her for a walk, a very slow walk, then went home and agonized for a while. Eventually, I decided to take her. That evening, I gave Peter two scotches and said I had something to tell him. "I know you're not pregnant," he said, "so you must have gotten a dog."

"How did you know?"

"You didn't, really. . . ."

"Well," I said, "if you don't like this dog, we won't get her, but I *am* getting a dog."

Peter: Lennie was all promises. I would never have to walk the dog, feed it, clean up after it, you know the routine. So finally I said, "If we have to have a dog, let's get this one. She needs a home."

Leni: We renamed her Thelma. At first, I spent a lot of time with her, and, naturally, she bonded with me. Peter felt left out; he said, "She doesn't like me."

I said, "She doesn't know you." Then I went out of town, and Thelma and Peter spent the day together. That was it. Now she goes everywhere with us.

Peter: If you're going to have a dog, you've got to have her with you. When we go to our house in the country for the weekend, Thelma goes with us in the helicopter and to Colorado in our plane when we go skiing.

Leni: She should have kept the name Princess.

Peter: She's very smart and adaptable. It's as if she's made a deal: "Just take me with you, and I won't be any trouble." We've become a real threesome.

Leni: Of course, Peter does all the things he said he would never do, and Thelma is a huge, wonderful addition to our lives.

Peter: Now, I would never want to be without a dog.

JOE

SUSAN DUNCAN

Coordinator, Delta Society National Service Dog Center

When I met Joe at the local humane society, he immediately knocked me down, spilling his water bowl, so I was not only flat on the ground but soaking wet. Not a good beginning, but later I accidentally dropped my cane, reached for Joe and leaned on him. He didn't move. I was a bit more impressed. Also, he had a kind, intelligent look, and he was large. I have multiple sclerosis and needed a large dog to help me walk. After that he never again even bumped me hard, and when I brought my daughters (ten and three) to meet him the next day, he was gentle and careful with them. I decided to take a chance on him.

Long before Joe came into my life, we had a family pet, Casper, a Samoyed/Lab cross from the humane society, a sweet dog who loved the children and let them dress him in birthday hats and sometimes even a tutu. He was a real gentleman, though certainly not trained for service work in any way. It had never occurred to me that a dog might be able to help me; but one day I fell down in the yard, couldn't get up and called Casper over for comfort. He licked my face, looked at me, then shoved his head under my shoulder, pushed me into a sitting position, and stood patiently as I managed to pull myself up while holding on to him. The way I see it, he actually volunteered his services.

From then on, Casper helped me walk, to get up when I fell, and carried things for me in his backpack. Then a tumor ended his life very suddenly. I was with him for the euthanasia and watched as he hung on for a long time—longer, the vet said, than any animal in his experience. Finally I said, "It's OK, Casper, I'll be OK." Then he closed his eyes and died.

I was devastated. I couldn't imagine ever having another dog until I realized that my husband and daughters were trying to substitute for Casper. I knew I had to regain the independence he had given me, so we brought Joe home. At first, he was totally undisciplined. It was a struggle for both of us. Joe needed attention, he needed boundaries, but, most of all, I think he needed a job.

Many times during the first few months I thought, This will never work. However, little by little, Joe learned to walk quietly beside me, to stay still to help me stand up, to retrieve my cane. Now he is an integral part of my day. In the morning he can pull back the bed covers, gently put my feet one at a time on the floor, help me in and out of the shower, open the refrigerator, give me a yogurt, open and close the dishwasher and pull out the racks, put clothes into the washer, take them out of the dryer and put them in a basket. His folding techniques are still a little haphazard. He can go with me to the supermarket, take items from the shelves and carry everything in his backpack. He helps me get in and out of the pool. He retrieves money from the cash machine. He understands more than 100 verbs and nouns, plus various combinations of words. After three years together, I find that we also communicate nonverbally. Joe will anticipate my needs; for instance, when I have trouble walking, I often find him right there at my first stumble. Maybe he sees this as part of his job description, but I think it's a manifestation of our strong emotional bond.

Love is not always instantaneous. In our case, it took six months to even get started, in part because I was determined to keep our relationship businesslike and unemotional. Obviously, we have gone way beyond that. We have a bond of trust and love which means everything to me and, apparently, to Joe as well. We are both much happier when we are together. After his evening walk with my husband, Joe always comes straight to me and rubs against me as if touching base.

I couldn't do the things I do without Joe; he gives me an independence I would otherwise never have. Joe loves a challenge, and that is probably the reason he sticks with me. I know that he will do virtually anything I ask, if I can only show him what I want.

HEIDI

FRED NAUMANN
Retired chemical engineer

SALLY NAUMANN
Housewife, not retired

When we heard that there was a German shepherd pup at our local shelter, we raced right out to see her. Heidi was about three months old and wanted to kiss any hand that came near. Her owner was in jail for a month; no one knew if he would reclaim her at the end of that time, so we took many trips out there to visit her. When the owner finally decided he didn't want to take her back and we knew we could adopt her, we were there at the shelter the moment it opened. We brought Heidi home, and she's been a joy ever since.

We took her to obedience classes where she did very well. She's become quite a social dog, and loves people and other dogs. She gets her leash and takes us for a walk every day. She's like a member of the family (a member of the family that you actually like). She has really responded to kindness. We've never met a more loving or gentler dog. She's just beautiful, a beautiful personality, a beautiful spirit.

BOY AND ALFIE

JENNIE MAYLE
Photographer

PETER MAYLE
Writer

Jennie: Boy came first. I found him on the roadside when we were living in France.

Peter: He was in a terrible condition. He was thin as a rail with almost no fur, and he had a severe thyroid problem which made his vision so bad he bumped into parked cars. His head seemed very heavy; he had to keep resting it on things. He has made a remarkable recovery. Now he's looking more and more like a large piece of hairy furniture.

He may be a griffon Korthals, an ancient and distinguished breed. Prince Rainier has one, so you can just imagine.

Boy has been in every magazine in Europe. He seems to be drawn by the sound of the shutter, and a photographer trying to get a shot of a house will find Boy firmly planted in the foreground.

Jennie: Then, when we were living in the United States, Alfie appeared. One summer I saw a lovely large shaggy dog in Run #12 at the pound. At the time we had an elderly Labrador and didn't want to upset her with a new dog. I kept an eye on him in the meantime, and eventually he was adopted. That winter I stopped in town one day to speak to three big dogs in the back of a truck. When the driver appeared, he told me that one of them was looking for a new home because the woman who had adopted him found him too boisterous. Then I realized he was the one I had loved from Run #12. I took him home with the understanding that I might have to bring him back if he didn't get on with Boy. I shouldn't have worried. They skittered around the sitting room all evening playing, and they're still playing today.

Peter: We named the new dog Alfie. He's a marvelous dog, but so greedy—a walking stomach.

Both dogs are a joy. They bring an enforced discipline into our lives with mandatory walks twice a day, a respite from the phone and the computer. They are endlessly fascinating to observe. One of the reasons I write as slowly as I do is that they're usually in the office with me.

They are always thrilled to see you, no matter how vile you've been. When we come home, they rush around, wag and bring toys. They want really just a small part of your time, and in return they give you everything.

Author's Note: Boy tells his own story as the narrator in A Dog's Life, *by Peter Mayle (Vintage Books, 1996).*

CORY

ANNE REAP
Barn manager

The kids wanted a puppy, so we went to the pound. We looked at every puppy in the place, and then I spotted Cory, an adult German shepherd who was just standing in his run watching us. He was the only dog there who wasn't barking, so when he seemed to like the kids, we took him home.

    The next day, he went to work with me and he was wild. I don't think he had ever been loose before. By the second day, you would have thought he had spent his whole life in a horse barn. He learns fast. He's a great dog. I only wish he wasn't already seven years old.

MOCCA

DAVID KELSO
Coffee slinger

Mocca was fifteen when she came to live with me. Her owners traveled all the time and couldn't keep her anymore. She needed me, and maybe I needed her.

She is old, seventeen now, but it's OK; I work a lot, she sleeps a lot. We take a walk every day, and she loves road trips. She sleeps on the front seat of the pickup or looks out the window.

When I come home at night and she's asleep, I always look to see if she's breathing. When she goes, it's going to be the biggest loss of my life.

WYATT

MARGARET BISHOP
Horse trainer

When my dog Willy died very unexpectedly, I was devastated. I couldn't even think about another dog. After a few months, I still missed Willy terribly, but I thought maybe a new dog would help me get over it, at least as much as you ever do get over it. I went to a shelter, but it must have been too soon because I left in tears. I just wanted Willy back.

Several months later, when my mom was visiting, I decided to try again. We went to another animal shelter, and there he was (not yet named Wyatt), curled up in his cage, so depressed he wouldn't even lift his head to look at us. An attendant brought him out of the cage to take him to an outside pen where we could visit with him, but he couldn't stand up on the vinyl floor; he slipped and slid, and finally collapsed, sprawled out and trembling. When the attendant picked him up, he didn't seem to mind. I thought that was the first good sign. Outside, he raced around and completely ignored us. There were several other dogs who were definitely more socialized, dogs Mom thought were better bets, but somehow this one appealed to me.

A few days later I came back with my husband to see the dog. He was still terrified of everything, and again raced around and ignored us; but when I knelt down, he immediately ran over, threw himself across my lap and looked up at me. What could I do?

We brought him home and gave him a name, some dinner and a bed. Now he's part of the family. He settled right in and got over most of his fears. He had probably never been anywhere or seen anything.

The best thing about him is the way he really loves me. You can tell.

TRAGEDY AND CINNABAR

DANIEL DOUGLAS
Student

When I was a baby, we adopted Tragedy, a stray. She is a good dog but pretty old now, so when I was ten and old enough to have my own dog, I decided to look for one who needed a home.

My mom and I went to a shelter where we saw lots of dogs. One was a friendly young dog who had been abandoned on the Massachusetts Turnpike. From the beginning, he seemed to like me and I liked him, but Mom said we should think it over for a day or two. After all, you are getting a dog for life. When this dog is as old as Tragedy is now, I will be twenty-six. It makes you think.

That afternoon, we went to another shelter and saw a cute little fat puppy. She was nice, but I kept thinking about the other dog and the way he had looked at me as if he wanted to stay with me. First thing the next day we went back and adopted him. I named him Cinnabar.

When he came to our house, he was very quiet and polite, almost as if he felt like a guest. I think he is more comfortable now. He likes to be with me, to run around and play or just to sleep near me when I do my homework. When I come home from school, he's always waiting for me.

Elise Lufkin

TEDDY

JAMIE LEE CURTIS
Actor

Teddy belonged to one of my closest friends, Rick, and his partner, George. Rick and George had two dogs: Teddy and his mother, Aza, a Lhasa apso. The dogs were always around, so I got to know them quite well. They played with my dog, Clark, a pound dog.

Both men died with AIDS, George first. He suffered terribly. It was a long, drawn-out death, and the dogs witnessed it day by day. A week after George died, Aza died too. It seemed as if she couldn't bear any more. Then, a year later, Rick got sick, and Teddy had to watch Rick die. When Rick was in the hospital toward the end, I took Teddy in to visit him. The little dog fell asleep on the bed with Rick's hand on him, and Rick asked me if I would take care of Teddy. I agreed without even asking my family. I just took Teddy home with me, knowing that my husband, Chris, and our daughter, Annie, would understand.

Teddy saw his whole family—his beloved owners and his mother—wiped out in two years. He saw the people he loved suffering, he saw them cared for by strangers in the house, he saw them taken away to the hospital, he saw them in the hospital, and he waited for them when they didn't return. After Rick's death Teddy developed a serious skin condition and became extremely lethargic. I really thought he wouldn't live, so I tried to prepare Annie for that possibility. We talked about all that he had been through.

Teddy was very depressed for almost a year, but he has great tenacity and an ability to hang on. We have a baby now, Tom, who insists on sharing Teddy's bed and who seems to have given the dog a new sense of life. Gradually, he's become spry and playful again. He's a lovely addition to our family.

SAMMY

JULIE DILLON ROBERTS
Residential developer

One Sunday seven years ago, I was at church with my husband and son when the minister announced that five puppies had been abandoned on the church doorstep and anyone interested could see them in the Sunday school room. I most definitely was not interested, but my son was, and my husband said those fateful words, "Let's just look. . . ."

They were tiny furballs. Sammy fit in the palm of my hand, and, somehow, I found myself a little later with her at a pet shop, since there was no vet available on Sunday. The pet store owner said, "This puppy is three or four weeks old, much too young to leave her mother. You must take her back right away." Good advice, but unfortunately not an option, so we bought some puppy formula, and Sammy had bottles every four hours around the clock for weeks.

She has always been totally healthy and very smart. She grew up as a city dog, but recently we've been spending vacations in the mountains, and she hikes, climbs rocks and swims across streams as if she had been doing it all her life. For some reason, she has absolutely no interest in balls or toys, so her golden retriever friend, Webster, thinks she might not actually be a real dog.

She's real enough for me. She's the best dog I've ever had.

MYRTLE AND LUCILLE

CHRIS KRESGE
Investor

JUSTIN BOGDANOVICH
Bookseller

Justin: We found Myrtle at a roadside stand in Michigan, where she had been abandoned with all her littermates. We almost took two puppies; they were all cute, and we didn't know anything about dogs, but fortunately, we decided on just one. It was Myrtle. She is an Irish setter/German shepherd cross, and as a puppy and young dog she was wildly hyperactive. We managed to civilize her a bit. At first, she listened only to Chris; now she's pretty obedient for both of us, at least most of the time.

Chris: Lucille appeared in my life one day when Justin brought her home from the shelter with a big bow around her neck and handed her to me. We were in the middle of a construction project, with the house and yard completely torn up. To add a puppy to the confusion and mess seemed insane, so I said, "She's really cute, but this is not a good time for us to get another dog. She will have to go back."

Justin: Within fifteen minutes, Chris had named her Lucille, after his favorite aunt.

Chris: Well, she needed a home, and somehow that seemed more important than the inconvenient timing. She had had a hard life; she and her sister were just dumped on the side of the highway in the middle of winter.

Justin: And look how nicely everything worked out.

Chris: It did work out, partly because Lucille was such a good puppy: calm, clean and well-behaved. She's a chow/shepherd mix. She looked like a little bear. Myrtle was very jealous at first and kept hoping we would come to our senses and send her back; now they're best friends.

Justin: Sometimes Lucille goes to the store with me, and Chris keeps Myrtle with him. I just dote on them. I take them for lots of walks, and, when I'm away, I miss them. They're like my kids.

Chris: The most special part of my relationship with the dogs is their companionship. They just like to be with you. When you come home and they look up and see you, they're happy.

SASHA

RACHEL PETERS
Costume designer

When I decided to get a dog, I wanted to really make a difference, perhaps save a life. I went to the big city pound where there were so many dogs that they are kept only a few days. It was an extremely disturbing experience for me. I certainly admire the people who have the courage to work there.

I walked through the place until I saw a dog who appealed to me, I'm not sure exactly why. They let her out of the cage. She was emaciated, with matted fur, and she smelled of urine; but when I lifted her hair, she had such kind eyes. I felt overwhelmed. I wanted to think it over, so I said to the attendant, "Let's put her back. I need to think about this." When we tried to put the dog back in the cage, she flattened herself on the floor, stretched out her four legs and resisted with all her strength. I couldn't stand it, so I said, "OK, I give up. I'll take her."

Later at home, I wondered what I had done. The dog stood there, trembling and scared; she looked horrible and smelled worse. I got right in the shower with her. The next day I took her to the vet and the groomer.

Today, Sasha is a different dog in every way. I was lucky. When you know nothing about a dog's background, you are definitely taking a chance. Some of these dogs have serious hang-ups, which is not surprising when you think of what they've been through.

Sasha is amazingly well-adjusted. She's very friendly; she likes people and other dogs. She takes me to the park every day. She likes to swim. She's very clean in the house, though she does love to roll in disgusting things, and she always wants to be hugged, smelly or not. Fortunately for both of us, my parents think Sasha is wonderful. My mother is usually thrilled when I go away, because they can keep her while I'm gone.

It's great to come home to her. What a welcome! She's a special, special dog.

ROBBIE JO, SHORDIE AND SADIE

GAIL GAFFNEY
Dog groomer

I have three adopted dogs. Robbie Jo is a Rottweiler/Doberman cross who was born blind. She was picked on by her littermates. (She still has the scars and has always been scared of puppies.) Her owner surrendered her to Animal Control; shortly after that, she and I found each other. She feels safe with me, at home and at work; but if a stranger comes in, she heads straight for her crate.

When Shordie was only twelve weeks old, his former owners moved out and abandoned him with only a blanket. He's still bonded to his blanket. I fostered him for the SPCA and ended up adopting him three weeks later. He's a real character and a show-off. He's kind of a traitor, actually; he falls in love with everyone.

I got Sadie, the poodle, when she was dropped from the hearing-dog program. (Sadie says she decided to make a career change, because she certainly could have done the work if she'd really wanted to.) She seems to like her new job as receptionist and cashier for the grooming business. She greets people, with help from Shordie, and collects the money. She takes cash or checks, but if a client is slow, she sometimes gets impatient and grabs the whole wallet to bring to me.

They give me so much love. Sometimes they just look at you, and it means everything.

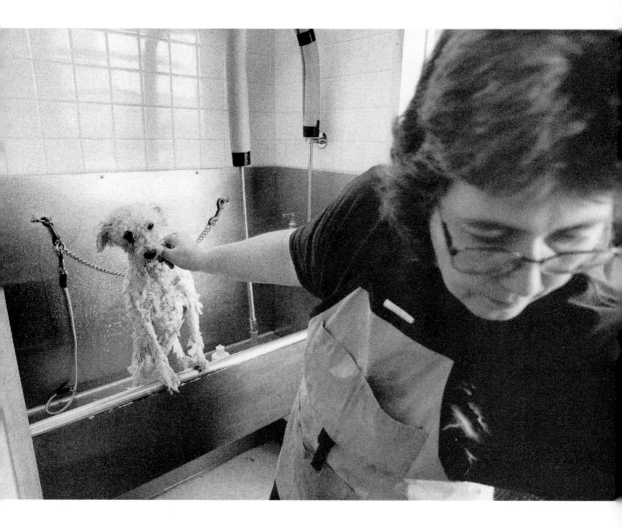

LUCY

JOSH WALTHER
Horse trainer

One year, just before Christmas, a friend called me from Canada. She was in a bowling alley and had clearly enjoyed a few beers. "Josh, I've found a dog for you, a skinny, beautiful redbone coonhound. She was in the muck heap behind the barn." I started out by saying, "Call me back in the morning when you make more sense," but finally—who knows why—I gave in and said, "Send her on down."

When I went to pick up the dog—that I didn't really want—at the air cargo depot, there was Lucy, cowering, completely traumatized, with tinsel around her neck. At home, I put her in a horse stall with food and water. The next day she was still freaked out; she escaped and disappeared for three days. I left food for her outside the barn, and she did start coming back to eat, but she lived in the woods. This went on for about three weeks. I started moving her food into the barn gradually, but she still wouldn't let me touch her. One day she came to my house, walked in, jumped on the sofa and went to sleep.

For a year or more, Lucy was very nervous and easily frightened. She hates thunderstorms. Once, when we were staying near an Air Force bombing range, she totally panicked and wedged herself under the deck so tightly she couldn't get out. We had to tear half the boards off to liberate her, and then she was anything but grateful.

Now, Lucy is well fed, shiny and sleek. She has always had beautiful ears; now, she will actually let me rub them. She's such a good judge of character that I have learned to trust her instincts. When she won't go near someone, I pay attention. Sometimes she looks as if she's listening to voices in her head. She may be a little crazy, but she's a happy dog, and I love her.

TIGRE

NINA BURLEIGH
Journalist

I first named her Tigre because she has stripes, but now that I know her better, I call her Gre, pronounced *gray*. Tigre seems way too cool for this dog.

I found her at a big city shelter in Chicago one cold rainy spring. The shelter had a window on the street, and in it I saw an odd-looking dog. She was tiger-striped, orange and brown, with white feet, long legs and a long tail. She was very skinny. I couldn't see her face; that was my excuse for going in. Besides, a short time before, I had found an abandoned dog at a rest stop on the highway, had left it there and still felt terrible about it.

I went into the shelter and asked to see the dog. When they brought her out, she jumped up and licked my face. She was very friendly. When she had first arrived at the shelter, she was given only a week to live, but her death sentence kept getting postponed, probably because she was so sweet.

I just *had* to adopt her, but when I first took her home, things were a little rough. My beagle was not happy at all. Gre was groggy and sick from being spayed, and then after she recovered, it took six months to house-train her. But she was so appealing and so devoted that it all seemed worthwhile.

She is a great companion. She simply wants to be with me. She even waits outside the bathroom door when I'm taking a shower. She makes me feel safe in this neighborhood because she seems to have a sixth sense for bad people. She loves children, and although many of the kids around here are afraid of dogs, Gre has such a kind heart and such gentle ways that she makes friends with most of them. Robert, shown here, is one of her best friends.

Her life before we met is a mystery. I would love to know her story: where she lived and with whom, how she became a stray, what wonderful mixture of breeds she is. I would never trade this dog for a purebred. Her personality and her odd-but-appealing looks are all part of her mutt heritage. I'm afraid she is a bit of a reverse snob. The only dog in the world she doesn't like is a standard poodle.

BOB GUTIERREZ

Animal behavior coordinator, San Francisco SPCA

She was a tough puppy, a real survivor. A homeless man on the pier sold her, when she was only four weeks old, for ten dollars to some German tourists with a soft spot for dogs. They soon realized that it was not very practical to continue their travels with a four-week-old puppy, and she ended up here at the SPCA. I agreed to provide a foster home for her since at that age she needed bottle feeding every four hours. I had recently moved to a place where I could have a dog and thought this would be an interesting trial run. I didn't name her because I didn't plan to keep her.

After three weeks she was ready to go back to the SPCA to be put up for adoption, but I realized then that I wasn't ready to let her leave my life.

I adopted her and gave her the name Alcina, which means "strong-minded one" in Greek. We did obedience work together. I took her to puppy classes to socialize her and discovered that she is highly social. Now I often use her at work to test dogs coming into the shelter to see how they get along with other dogs. Alcina is not put off if a dog snaps or growls; she just sits there. She tests cats, too, to see if they like or will even tolerate dogs.

Alcina is a working dog. As part of our animal-assisted therapy program, she goes to hospitals, burn units and homes for the elderly. A volunteer took Alcina to visit coma patients when she first started working in the program. In less than forty-five minutes the dog was back in my office, a failure because she wouldn't stay on the beds! She knew she wasn't supposed to be on beds. It took me almost two weeks to train her to get on a bed and stay there. It was a little confusing at first, but she picked it up pretty quickly.

She's good at reading people. In the pediatric burn unit that she visits, some of the kids are active and some are quiet. Alcina takes cues from them and adjusts her program. Sometimes she races around with a ball; sometimes she just snuggles up quietly with a young patient.

Alcina has a talent for training puppies. She has raised a very nice Rottweiler, also from the SPCA, and is now working on a Belgian malinois.

I think that she is a mixture of golden retriever, Australian shepherd and German shepherd. Look at that face. It takes me forty-five minutes every morning just to put on the eyeliner.

I tend to connect my dogs to the times they see me through, both the good and the difficult times. In three years this puppy has gone from homeless to priceless.

CHARLIE

BUNNY WILLIAMS
Interior designer

Charlie was abandoned in a Bronx apartment when his owners moved and left him behind. The building super, who had already adopted five dogs, took him to the Humane Society where I met him.

I loved his face immediately, but he was much larger and considerably more rambunctious than the dog I had imagined sharing city life with me and my Norfolk terrier, Brewster. However, Charlie had his own agenda. After only a few minutes in the get-acquainted area, he came right over and put his head in my lap. Then he raced off again to play. I was weakening fast, but still trying to concentrate on another dog in the room, one that was considerably smaller and quieter. The next thing I knew, Charlie came flying over and landed right on my lap. At that point, I knew it was all over.

Though I did go home alone that day with the sensible idea of thinking it over for twenty-four hours, I came right back the next morning to adopt Charlie. My life has never been the same. He has been a handful at times, but he is one of the most attentive and affectionate dogs I have ever known. He wants to be with me constantly, and he is never indifferent.

It seems to me that when a neglected dog is finally given love and attention, he will be incredibly grateful. Charlie certainly is. He shows it with wild excitement when I come home and by snuggling up quietly when I'm tired or sad. He gives me so much; actually, I'm the lucky one.

JETT, MOMMER DOG, KELLY AND MAGGIE

FLO OXLEY

Programs manager and botanist,
National Wildflower Research Center

On my way to work one foggy morning, I almost ran over two dogs. They just materialized out of the mist. They were basically skeletons, a black and white skeleton (that's Mommer Dog), and a large, completely black skeleton (that's Jett). Later that morning, I took them to the vet, and we discovered they were also badly infected with scabies. They had to stay at the vet's for a month to get rid of the scabies, fatten up and find a home. I visited them every day, so it wasn't much of a surprise to anyone when they went home with me at the end of that month.

We already had Kelly, the golden retriever. She doesn't have a dramatic story; she just needed a home because her owner couldn't keep her, and we gave her one.

Maggie, the little black one, turned up one day on the side of the road. My husband, Bill, thought he saw something behind a beer can as we were driving by; he looked in the rear view mirror, and the something moved. We went back, and there was Maggie, a tiny pup.

They are all tremendously affectionate; it's like a party every time I come home. They know they're special, they know they've got me wrapped around their paws, and I hope they know they never have to worry again.

TIKI

KATHY THOMPSON
Health education specialist

I have had seizures for twenty-nine years. Four years ago, I heard about seizure-alert dogs—dogs who can sense a seizure before the affected person realizes one is coming on and are trained to warn their owners. I applied to the Purdy Prison Pet Partnership program, where inmates train animals from shelters to be service dogs. Eventually they introduced me to Tiki, a two-year-old border collie/samoyed/shepherd mix from an animal shelter. Tiki had done obedience work and general service dog training at the prison; I joined her there to learn how we could work together. The instructors say they wish the people were as easy to teach as the dogs. Anyway, we graduated together.

Some dogs can detect a coming seizure, perhaps by scent, perhaps by changes in breathing patterns, but no one knows for sure how they do it. Tiki will whimper or howl softly to warn me so I have time to get to a safe place and sit down. Then she stays right next to me during the seizure. She is not only intelligent, but so sensitive. She usually licks my hand to comfort me because the seizures can be very, very scary. She likes people, and she loves my husband, Kelly, but she and I have something special. We are completely tuned in to each other. I wish I had found her years ago.

CINDY LOU

BILL BERLONI
Theatrical animal trainer

The dog I trained for the role of Sandy in the original production of *Annie* years ago came from a shelter. Ever since then I have been known in the local shelters as the guy who takes Sandy dogs. One day I got a call about Cindy Lou, a stray who must have been on the streets a long time because she had a collar embedded in her neck. When the poor dog got to the shelter, the collar had to be surgically removed (she still has a half-inch scar).

Cindy Lou was indeed a Sandy dog, but a badly abused one and extremely shy. Even though I was sure she would never perform, I took her with the hope of rehabilitating her enough to find her a good home. It was a slow process, but she improved; and when I had to go on the road with the preopening run of *Annie Warbucks*, I took Cindy Lou along as understudy. To my amazement, I realized during the tour that she was better than the dog we had in the role; ultimately, she finished the run and opened the New York production. She performed at the White House with the cast of *Annie Warbucks* and recently appeared in the Steve Martin film *Mixed Nuts*. She has toured the country playing Sandy in productions of *Annie* and *Annie Warbucks* and is currently performing on Broadway in the twentieth anniversary revival of *Annie*.

My home is a Grand Central Station for unwanted animals. I have nine permanent dogs: two who are impossible to place and seven workers like Cindy Lou who help me in a profession that helps support all of us. Cindy Lou is a star, but she's also just my dog and a real pet.

DONNA-CARRIE

TERRY SUGGS
Owner, Capitol Signs Incorporated

One day a humane officer was driving through town when she noticed a big guy waving a big stick and chasing a terrier. She pulled over to ask the man what he was doing. He explained that he was going to beat the dog because she wouldn't come when he called. He said that he kept her chained to the stair railing behind his apartment, that kids must have untied her and that many beatings had not taught her to come back when called because she was too dumb. When the officer told him about the anticruelty code, which prohibits beating and cruel confinement, the man decided that he didn't want her any more. The officer, who knew that the city shelter was so overcrowded that the dog would have to be euthanized, took her to a neighbor of mine, Linda, who often finds homes for dogs that have been abused, neglected or abandoned.

Linda called me because she knew that my fiancée, Jacquie, and I were looking for a dog. We had decided that we didn't want to take just any dog. We wanted a dog who really needed us. We wanted to save a life. We had been told that a dog would come to us, so when Linda called to tell me about the terrier, I knew right away that this was our dog. I was at work at the time, but Jacquie went over immediately to see the dog, loved her and brought her home.

We named her Donna-Carrie. She was a little timid, but she soon got over that. At first I couldn't get her to do anything. She just looked at me as if she had no idea what I was talking about. We took her to obedience training classes. The trainer spoke to the dogs in Japanese, and Donna-Carrie seemed to understand every word. Now we use Japanese words for sit, stay, come and other commands. I guess we were not speaking her language, though why her language should be Japanese I don't know. She also understands English now.

She often goes to work with me. When she first came to us, I brought her to work every day because she was not completely house-trained. When she seemed settled enough to leave at home, I told her the night before, "Tomorrow is a big day for you. You're going to stay home. I have complete confidence in you. I know you'll be good."

Usually in the morning Donna-Carrie waited by the door, all set to lead me out to go to work, but that day she sat on her bed and watched me get ready. Before I left I said, "Remember, I have faith in you. Now come and give me a kiss." She came over, gave me a little kiss and went back to her bed. I left for work, and when I came home, actually a little early, she greeted me with excitement. Then she went outside and urinated for a long time. The house was perfect.

She's a dog with a great personality. She knows she has a wonderful home. She loves Jacquie because Jacquie plays with her and carries on. They have long conversations; Jacquie speaks in her own voice and then answers in Donna-Carrie's voice. They both enjoy this, and I must say that it's pretty entertaining.

When Donna-Carrie first came home with us, I had some serious trouble with allergies, but now I take something that helps keep things under control. Originally the allergist suggested that I should give up the dog, but I said, "No way! I saved this dog, and I will not give her up."

GRACE

HOLLY BETH ECKHARDT
Bookstore owner

When I saw an ad for two-month-old collie/Lab puppies at a private shelter, I went to look at them. The shelter was actually in someone's house and a big barn out back. The barn was full of cages, and there were puppies in drawers and closets. When the man there brought Grace out for me to see, she escaped and hid under my car. It took almost an hour to coax her to come out.

After I took her home, four days passed before she would let me get near her; but ever since then, she has been totally attached. She goes everywhere with me; at least, she does when she wants to. In the morning when I leave for work, I ask her if she wants to go to the bookstore. Either she runs over and jumps in the car, or she stays on the porch. *She* decides.

Grace means everything to me. When I'm sad, she jumps up and sits close to me. She is absolutely and completely my best friend.

JULIO

JANET ABROMEIT
Speech therapist

DOUG ABROMEIT
Director,
National Avalanche Center

Janet: One summer, when I was working in the mountains for the U.S. Forest Service checking sheepherder permits for grazing, I started talking to a herder and noticed two small puppies with his dogs. He told me his boss would allow him to keep only one of the puppies. He had killed all the females when they were tiny and had kept these two males to see which one seemed more likely to be a useful herding dog. He had chosen one and planned to shoot the other, perhaps the next day. He said he was sick about it, but being up in the mountains with the sheep, he couldn't find homes for the pups. Julio—my Julio, the big furball—was the expendable one.

Well, of course, in no time he was mine to take home to Doug, who was quite surprised. I must admit I was surprised myself. I had forgotten all the training you have to do with a puppy. We were lucky though; our neighbor's golden retriever came to inspect our new addition and decided to take over Julio's care and training. Julio curled right up with her, happy as can be, and for months he followed her everywhere. The retriever was a great role model, but Julio was a tough puppy: stubborn and very, very smart. As an adolescent about a year old, he was pretty wild and always testing us.

Doug: At that time we moved to the mountains and started training him for avalanche rescue. He caught on really fast; as soon as he learned the word *search*, he would sniff the air and start digging, always in the right place. It seemed as if having a job helped him to settle down. He's twelve now, but he still goes out with us when we're skiing in the backcountry, although we do have to be more selective about where we take him now that he's getting older. He's a good outdoor partner, a real companion. He loves camping; he likes to sleep out next to the tent. When we're hiking, he herds us, checking back with us and going from one to the other. He definitely likes his whole group together.

Janet: He just loves life. When he was a puppy, he would leap in the air to catch snowflakes, and that image seems to me to describe his personality. He's pretty sweet, a happy old guy. He's been a really good friend.

BLAZER

JONATHAN BEARDSLEY
Carpenter

I had been looking for a Dalmatian for a long time when I heard of a puppy in a shelter in Pennsylvania. He was only eight weeks old, but the breeder had decided that he was unusually small, a runt in fact, and had turned him over to the shelter. I drove out there to see him before I made the decision to adopt, partly because some Dalmatians have a genetic tendency toward deafness. He was fine, so I took him home.

He was not an easy puppy to raise. He was excitable, hard to train and into everything. He ate some poison and nearly died. He grew up to be a perfectly normal size and a beautiful dog. I continued to work on his training. Now he's well behaved and a pleasure to be around. He comes to work with me unless it's very cold. He can climb ladders, but I don't encourage it. It's too dangerous. He gives his paw to shake, either right or left. He's a good house dog. He does like to sleep on the couch, which is really fine with me.

When my wife and I got divorced, Blazer chose me. He's a great companion.

MAGNETO

JULIE CLARK
Airline pilot and air show performer

In April, 1985, I was a new airline captain with a crew on a layover in International Falls, Minnesota. It was snowing that morning as we were about to leave for the airport. The copilot noticed a little shaggy dog outside, snow melting on its black fur. As I opened the door, the dog scurried off. The guy at the reception desk said, "That damn dog has been hanging around for four days. The guests feed her; she comes and goes."

It was time to leave for the airport. I boarded the van with the rest of the crew and some passengers for my flight. As we pulled into the street, the driver said, "There's that crazy dog. It's been stopping traffic standing in the road."

Without really thinking, I said, "We've got to go back to the hotel."

The van driver protested, but when I explained to the passengers that I was their pilot and guaranteed that they wouldn't be late for their connections, we turned around. When we got back to the hotel, there was no dog in sight. I looked around and then spotted this little black thing running behind a parked car. I chased her through the icy parking lot, slipping and skating until I finally caught her. The poor dog was just a puppy, maybe four months old. She was shaking, scared, wet and cold, and she stank.

We got back in the van and headed off to the airport, where we made our flight with time to spare, much to my relief. I took the dog into the cockpit with me. It was very noisy up there, and she was scared, so while the copilot flew his designated leg, I held the dog, trying to warm her up. It was a short flight, but by the time we landed, the puppy had attached herself to me. I think even then she saw me as her protector.

The next day, I called in sick for work, stuffed a fifteen-pound dog in a pet carrier designed for a seven-pound cat, and took her home to California. I named her Magneto, Mags for short. I think she's a cockapoo terrier.

From the beginning, Mags always wanted to be near me. She never ran off. She's a one-person dog and the kid I never had. I don't know if any other dog could have adapted to my lifestyle the way she has. All summer we're on the circuit doing aerobatics at air shows. Mags is known as the Flying Dog, or Magneto Aero Dog. We've been on TV. She wears earplugs, of course, and she always seems happy to get on the plane. As long as she's with me, she'll go anywhere.

JETT

PHYLLIS BICKERSTAFF
Human developmentalist

Our son, Jefferson, brain-injured at birth, has impaired motor skills. When Jefferson was eight, my husband, Mac, and I learned of Canine Assistants, a new organization in our area that provides dogs to help people with disabilities. We were particularly interested in this group because they use humane training methods and work only with dogs from shelters.

When Jefferson and I went out to the facility to see the dogs in training, we were greeted by a border collie named Lucy who gave us brochures and a few minutes later presented us with more brochures. Then she gave Jefferson a quick kiss. A little later a large black Lab came over to welcome us; eventually we met the rest of the dogs in the training program. Jefferson was delighted and not a bit afraid of the dogs even though he was on the floor and they were looming above him.

I filled out an application form although we had no idea how long it would take to get a dog. Canine Assistants, even in its early days, had a waiting list and very strict criteria for people applying for one of their dogs. Then as now, a candidate must demonstrate need as well as the means and ability to care for the dog inside the house, more or less as a member of the family.

When we left, Jefferson was excited and hopeful. Lucy gave us some more brochures.

Several months later, Jennifer, the director of Canine Assistants, called to say that she might have a dog for Jefferson. At a local shelter she had found Smoky, a Lab mix who passed all the tests for temperament and willingness to work. He seemed like a perfect candidate. "But," she said, "don't tell Jefferson yet, because there is one problem." Smoky had a very serious case of parvovirus, which was discovered only after Jennifer had adopted him. He was now in an animal hospital, and the vet there said it would be at least a week before they knew if Smoky would even survive. It was a very long week, but by the end of it he seemed a little better.

At that point we decided to tell Jefferson about the dog. He started thinking of names. He particularly liked Jett as in jet-black or jet plane, and his great grandfather's name was Jett McCoy Bickerstaff. Jefferson liked the name Smoky, too, and thought the dog might like to keep his original name, so we decided to call him Jett Smoky Bickerstaff. We laid in a supply of toys and made a sign that said Smoky's New Home. Finally Jefferson and I went to the animal hospital to see the dog. When the vet brought him out, emaciated and still wobbly from the parvo, Jefferson was on the floor. He looked up at the dog. The dog looked at him and then came over and licked his face. Jefferson put his arms around him. The two seemed to have a common bond: Each had a difficult time staying in the world, each through no fault of his own.

After almost eight weeks Jett was strong enough to start his training program with Canine Assistants. We went every week to visit him. Six months later, Jett was ready to settle in at our house and go to work. He turns on lights, retrieves things and opens doors, but his most important job is simply being Jefferson's best friend.

Canine Assistants asks that, in return for a service dog, you give time back to the community. Jefferson and his dad go to the Canine Assistants training facility every Sunday to feed the dogs and horses and to clean stalls. We take Jett to visit at a nearby home for older folks, and when Jefferson goes for physical therapy, Jett comes along and works with the other children. When they do their exercises, they get to shake hands with Jett or hug him as a reward. Sometimes, when the exercises are difficult or painful, he will lick their tears.

Although Jett goes almost everywhere with Jefferson (to Boy Scouts, restaurants, or movies), he does stay home when Jefferson goes to water therapy. Then he just sits by the door and waits for Jefferson's return. Although I feed him and take him out, Jefferson is definitely the most important person in his life.

Jett's greatest contribution is the way he helps to remove the stigma of Jefferson's disability. People see that Jett loves Jefferson dearly. Other kids are more interested in Jett and the way he will shake hands or retrieve than they are in the fact that Jefferson is creeping on his hands and knees instead of walking. You would have to see Jett and Jefferson together at Boy Scouts to realize how this works. Every day Jett helps Jefferson cope with the loneliness of being different.

BILLY AND SKYLAND FARM

Billy found Twister, the big black and white dog, seventeen years ago wandering around at a Grateful Dead concert. Later that year, he found Smiley half dead somewhere next to a dumpster. The vet thought she had probably been attacked by a bunch of dogs. Both dogs lived with Billy for a number of years. They used to come out here to the barn at Skyland farm with him when he came to ride his horses.

When Billy died a few years ago, the barn just took the dogs in. We started a Dog Fund for food and medical expenses. Twister had a little stroke last year; you can see how he still weaves a bit when he walks. We all chip in to take care of them. They are sweet dogs, and we're glad to do it, for them and for Billy.

NOELIA

PERRY HABERMAN
Manager, Madison Avenue Bookshop

Noelia decided to adopt me when we met in a cafe on the island of Ibiza off the coast of Spain. On the first day of a week of backpacking and exploring, I stopped for a sandwich and was immediately approached by a small stray puppy with enormous ears. She was working the room and apparently had decided to concentrate on me. I shared my sandwich with her, and for the next week she followed me everywhere, scrambling through the cliffs along the coast, snuggling up when I stopped to rest and read.

On the last day, when I started hitchhiking back toward the airport, a truck stopped for me. I looked at Noelia and thought, I can jump on the truck and drive away, probably the sensible thing to do, or I can pick her up and take her with me. Of course, I picked her up, and here she is, still with me. For twelve years we have traveled and lived all over the world—Barcelona, Paris, the Philippines, and now New York and the bookstore. I think Noelia gives a good feeling to the place.

Through many different turns in my life, Noelia has been a constant friend.

NICKY

CANDY HERMAN
Travel agent

Several years ago, I watched a National Geographic special on racing greyhounds. I was horrified by the piles of corpses, dogs destroyed because they were no longer at the peak of their racing ability. Those greyhounds haunted me for a long time, and I began to seriously consider rescuing one. My husband agreed (though he really wanted a vizsla for hunting), so I finally decided to do it.

I contacted Greyhound Pets of America, whose representative interviewed us to make sure we understood the responsibility involved and were prepared to undertake it. Greyhounds can never run loose. Their sight is much better than humans' or other dogs', so something moving far away can trigger their running instinct. They are so fast they can be in the next county before they stop.

Anyway, we qualified, and I went to the airport to meet Nicky, or Dixie Girl, as she was known in her old life at the racetrack. She was three years old, about average racing retirement age. When I saw her, I started to cry, thinking about what her future might have been. At first, she was very timid. Her life had been so limited; she had never seen stairs, glass doors, bikes, kids' toys—or kids, for that matter. She was terrified of our two cats, who were happy to encourage this fear. (She had been cat tested for our situation because some greyhounds can be aggressive with small animals, a natural instinct.)

The first six months were tough for all of us, but then she settled down and seemed to feel at home. She's an easy dog; she sleeps most of the day. She doesn't need a lot of exercise, but she loves to go for a walk (on a leash, of course). She's quiet and gentle. You can tell she appreciates anything you do for her. She's my girl, definitely my dog, and it makes me happy to know I could give her a life when she, like so many greyhounds all over the country, could easily have ended up part of a pile of corpses.

DAISY

AL GORE
Vice President of the United States

One summer a couple of years ago, I was vacationing with my wife, Tipper, and our four kids. We were staying on a friend's houseboat at Center Hill Lake in Tennessee. It was early evening, and our son, Albert, was out on a jet ski exploring the limestone bluffs around the lake. There are caves and all kinds of nooks and crannies with great potential for treasure hunting. Suddenly, Albert came racing back to the boat, yelling, "I've found a dog, and I think it's dying!"

His mother got on the jet ski with him, and together they went back to the dog. The dog was a pitiful sight, skin and bones. She could barely walk; her hind legs kept collapsing. Albert managed to load her onto the jet ski and hold her there for the trip back to the houseboat. She certainly looked pathetic, but we fed her a good meal and took her off to a veterinarian. He told us that she had a broken pelvis and had probably been abused.

We brought her back to the boat, nursed her and fed her, and, two days later, she was with us on Air Force Two heading back to Washington. She settled right in at our house and made friends with our other two dogs. Eventually her wounds healed. She began to walk and then to run. Now she's my jogging companion. We named her Daisy, though the kids often call her Inspector Turnip. She's a great little shaggy dog, and we all love her.

EDDY

GWEN CARLSON
Interior designer

We had been looking for a shih tzu when I noticed an ad for one at the local animal shelter. I certainly didn't expect to find a shih tzu at a shelter, but my husband and I went right over to see the little dog, and we really liked him.

His former owner had a history of drug and alcohol problems. One very cold winter night he left the dog tied up outside a local bar, apparently forgot about him and went home. Some kind soul rescued him that night and took him the next day to the shelter. He had a collar with a name tag, so the staff there called his owner, who never returned the calls. Maybe he thought the dog would be better off with someone else, who knows? He must have been kindly treated because he's so sweet and really very well trained. He lets us know exactly what he wants. He'll come and bark once, just a polite little bark; then, if he already has food and water, you'll know that he wants to go out. He will also bark for a treat, but, again, very politely.

Eddy was a scrawny, little tough guy when we got him. I guess he had to be tough to hold his own with all those big dogs at the shelter. He's definitely not intimidated by any dog, no matter how large; he's all bravado.

Eddy is a great dog, probably the easiest we've ever had. Everybody who meets him wants a dog just like him. He has to be involved in everything. When we give a party, he's usually in the middle of it. He's a funny little thing, a great little guy.

MORTIMER

PATRICIA LANDEGREN

Full-time mother of triplets

ERIK LANDEGREN

Chef/chocolatier

Erik: I wanted a dog for Patricia's birthday. I had heard about a vet in New York who sometimes places homeless dogs, so I called her and arranged a visit.

Patricia: When we got there, we were shown a scruffy, frightened black dog. He was very thin. He weighed only thirty-five pounds; now he weighs seventy, and he's not at all fat. A flight attendant had found him tied to a fence at La Guardia Airport and had brought him to the vet. He had definitely been kicked and beaten. He was terrified of any sudden movements or loud noises.

The vet suggested taking him on a trial basis, so we named him Mortimer and took him home.

The first two weeks were hard. If you lifted a hand to brush your hair, he cowered.

Erik: One day I took a golf club from the closet, planning to go outside to practice. Poor Mortimer looked at me in horror, ran to the other end of the house and shrank up like a little ball in a corner. He wouldn't come near me for hours afterwards. We had to spend lots of time with Mortimer, trying to gain his confidence. I jogged with him and took him everywhere with me. He needed to experience consistent kindness day after day for months before he knew he could trust us. Eventually he even let me rub his back with a golf club, and now he actually enjoys it.

Patricia: Mortimer today is a terrific dog. He's great with the kids, although sometimes he looks a little nervous when all three corner him. They pet him their way, but we try to make sure that they're always gentle.

Erik: Mortimer and I are very close. I speak Swedish to him and to the kids. He helps me get out to jog because I make a special effort not to disappoint him. He is a totally different dog now. I think he went from hell to heaven. He's completely a part of the family, and he has added so much to our lives. He gives us pleasure, peace and love.

AMANDA

KARLEENA HILLS
Computer graphics artist

When I first saw Amanda at the animal shelter, I knew I would love her. She's a poodle mix, and my favorite dogs had always been poodles. The last two were twins who were constantly with me. At night I slept with a poodle on each side of me; they packed me in like a sardine. When I moved to this apartment, I had to give them away, and I missed them terribly.

Because I have cerebral palsy and have trouble moving around, I wanted a service dog to give me some independence, to pick things up, and, most of all, for company and love. A law enacted in 1996, the Department of Housing and Urban Development "Pet Rule," provides specific protection for individuals with disabilities in government-subsidized housing who require service animals or pets. This rule also applies to the elderly. It came too late for my twin poodles, but not for Amanda.

Sue, the trainer who was to work with Amanda, came with me to the shelter to evaluate her. She thought the dog seemed intelligent, willing and very motivated by food and toys, useful for training. When we decided to take Amanda, the shelter attendant said, "That's good luck. Her time would have been up tomorrow." But I knew it was more than luck, because I, and everyone in my church, had been praying for a dog for me.

After months of hard work with Sue, Amanda came to live with me. At first I had trouble getting her to mind, because she was smart enough to know I couldn't do much to correct her. She's pretty good now. She answers the phone by pressing a button, opens doors by tugging on a towel tied to the handle, and picks things up when I drop them. She waits patiently until I can manage to take something from her, and if I drop it again, she rushes to pick it up with her tail wagging.

Last Thanksgiving at my brother's, Amanda went out on the patio after dinner and discovered a container full of turkey set out to cool. By the time we went to call her in, the turkey was gone. My brother and sister-in-law were not very happy, but I thought it was pretty smart of Amanda to open the tight lid on that container. She's very intelligent, funny and loving.

QUINCEY

ALISON LUFKIN
Interior decorator and antiques dealer

Quincey was a birthday present I gave to myself. For several years I have volunteered as an adoption counselor at the SPCA, so I see many, many dogs who need homes. I thought seriously about adoption for almost a year. I talked with dog trainers, with the staff at the SPCA and with every dog owner and dog lover I know. I researched the pros and cons of various breeds and mixed breeds, of males and females and of various temperaments and predispositions. I thought a lot about what kind of a dog would best fit into my life. I wanted a fairly mellow dog, probably a female, a dog who would get along with my two male corgis, Sullivan and Wiley. I wanted a dog who would enjoy long hikes. I wanted an adult because Wiley's puppyhood three years before had cured me of yearning for a puppy.

Whenever I worked at the shelter, I kept an eye out for my dog. People on the staff kept me posted on possibilities. A nice, friendly Doberman mix came in. I liked her very much, but when I brought the corgis in to meet her, she wanted to be the dominant dog, and they said, "No way! We hate her." Later I introduced them to a Rottweiler mix, but they thought she was too rambunctious.

Then one day I saw Quincey and fell totally in love with her. She was seven months old, very sweet, friendly and a little submissive. She had been picked up with two pit bulls on the Oakland-Alameda Bridge. At the SPCA she had passed both temperament and health tests. Her good health was particularly appealing because Sullivan has chronic back trouble and Wiley has serious, painful skin allergies and arthritis. I loved her looks. She is beautiful, probably part boxer, part pit bull and heaven only knows what else. I played with her a little, walked her around and spent some time sitting with her quietly. She seemed perfect for me. I brought Sullivan and Wiley to see her. She loved them immediately, but they were quite indifferent, which I took as a vote of approval. Now I pretend that the corgis fell in love too, but that is definitely an overstatement, although they do love her now.

I filled out the adoption papers, and we went home. I knew that I had done all the homework and reached a good, sensible decision. Still, I felt a little apprehensive, and I was right. The next few months were hell. The very first day Quincey ripped out the stitches from her spay surgery, so I had to rush her in for staples. She developed a serious though temporary skin problem. Sullivan went into depression. He snarled at Quincey and refused to speak to me. Wiley played with her at first, but when Sullivan finally began to accept her, Wiley, who by then was having a bout with arthritis, decided that he hated her.

I felt overwhelmed. I wondered whether Quincey would ever learn to behave. I took her to obedience classes and worked on her training at home. I gave her lots of exercise, which was a tremendous help. Gradually, she began to settle down. It must have been a big adjustment for her. Now she's great. She is sweet, loving and quite well behaved. We have continued the obedience classes, and I am thinking of trying agility training with her.

Quincey is a funny dog. Her antics make me laugh. I like the sense of connection I have with my dogs. I am always communicating with them in one way or another, and they with me.

Quincey loves every dog and every person who comes along, but most of all she loves me.

BOY

JOHN ROSSELLI
Antiques dealer

One cold November morning I thought I heard the sound of yelping out by the gate. I went down to investigate and found a very frightened puppy, who must have been thrown over the fence. He certainly wasn't too happy about it at the time, but in retrospect, I'm sure he thinks it was his lucky day.

Boy has been with me now for nine years. He sleeps under my bed and seems to love his life here, even knee-deep in whippets. He's a good boy!

MAX

LIZ COCHRANE
Stable manager

Before he found me, Max was known in the neighborhood as Hobo. He had spent a couple of years wandering between different farms; people at each place left food out for him. Eventually, we moved into that area, and one day Max showed up at our barn. I think he must have sensed that I needed him (and I did), because he made it quite clear from the start that he was not leaving. Once or twice a week he liked to visit his old friends, but as soon as he heard my car, he would run out and jump in for the ride home.

Max has been totally loyal to me from minute number one, but he's friendly to everyone, and everyone seems to respond to him. He's good at communicating what he wants. He will stare intently at a door, willing it to open (often it does), or at a potato chip, willing it to fall into his mouth (often it does). I don't know how he came to be a stray; I can't imagine anyone letting him go. I certainly could never have a better friend.

A woman we see once in a while on the circuit used to say, "I only wish my husband would look at me the way Max looks at Liz!"

DEALER

KEVIN WIGGINS
Carpenter

Dealer spent the first year of his life on a chain. He never had a chance to be a puppy. My girlfriend talked his owners into giving him to her when he was about a year old. They never cared about him anyway. My girlfriend was good to him, but her father was not. He was kind of rough with the dog. Then the family moved away, and Dealer was left with the grandmother. She was just keeping him, not really taking care of him, and once again he was neglected. The grandmother was a little senile and often forgot to feed him.

When he came to me five years ago, he weighed forty pounds; now he weighs seventy. He didn't take to me right away. He was so accustomed to not getting any attention that he didn't know what to do about it when he got some. It was frustrating in the beginning when he used to run off and just wouldn't listen to me. People say that you can't teach an old dog new tricks, but Dealer learned to recognize his name and to come when I call, most of the time. He understands the word "stay." He comes to work with me every day. He's busy in the winter; he likes to bury bones and food in the snow, probably in case he's ever really hungry again.

Now he's my best buddy, and if I hadn't taken him, he'd be on a chain today, he'd be . . . who knows where he'd be?

MINNIE

ANNE ADDINGTON
Psychologist

When my beloved golden retriever died very suddenly, I went into deep mourning. I eventually came out of it, but Bruno, my other golden, didn't. He lost his spunk; he was totally depressed.

One day I wandered into a pet store. Suddenly, it dawned on me that I had to get another dog. I asked the clerk where the nearest shelter was. He did give me a funny look, and then very kindly found an address for me. I went immediately to the shelter, but didn't see any dog that seemed right for me.

A few days later, I went to the SPCA, where I filled out the longest application I have ever seen. I was led through rooms of cages, finally ending up in the small dog department. When I saw Minnie, a stray picked up on the streets, she looked me right in the eye. When I gazed at that face, there was such a sweetness looking up. I fell in love immediately.

I took Minnie home with me, of course, and she thanks me every day for saving her. She sleeps on my bed with her head on a pillow. Bruno loves her. When I threaten to leave her in the park if she won't come, he refuses to go. When I pretend to walk away, he just sits down and won't move until she's with us again.

She is very athletic. She jumps like a cat; she's fascinating to watch. Perhaps she's part fox. She's smart too. She loves small children. When she plays with them, she gets very excited, but she seems to know when she's getting too excited. Then she just heads for her crate.

Minnie is extremely affectionate. All my dogs, past and present, are affectionate. How could they be anything else? They get so much love.

EMILY

ANNE COX CHAMBERS
Chairman,
Atlanta Newspapers

I opened the paper one morning eleven years ago and saw that the Pet of the Week for the Atlanta Humane Society was a beautiful, eighteen-month-old English sheepdog mix named Emily. Oddly enough, at the time one of my closest friends was very ill. Her name was Emily too.

I adopted Emily, Pet of the Week. She was lovely and still is; she is far more photogenic than I. She has always been good, a wonderful, wonderful companion. She has loved me completely.

P. PIE

HILLEARY BOGLEY
Humane foundation administrator

When I was thirteen, my mom came home one day with a cute little dog she had adopted from the local humane society. We named him P. Pie, which is short for your favorite kind of pie, whatever that may be. He had been seized by the authorities from a house where he'd been kept on a chain, living in an oil drum. His companions, cats sleeping in paint cans, were picked up at the same time, and some of them came to our house with P. Pie. My mom was always bringing animals home, but I felt there was something special about this dog. He walked in the door and ran right over to me. We bonded instantly. Sometimes that happens when you're very lucky.

Now I'm thirty-four, so that means P. Pie must be at least twenty-something. I wish he was only thirteen or fourteen, but really, he's in great shape. One of his back legs was injured and won't bend, but he gets around very well. He is blind, so when I move the furniture, it makes him mad. He has only one tooth, but he eats well, and he makes sure that all the other dogs respect him; he doesn't hesitate to growl at them if he thinks they're being fresh. Just the other day I heard a commotion and found him hanging off the neck of my poor rescued Rottweiler, Monster. Monster was horrified.

All my life I had dreamed of starting my own shelter. A few years ago I actually did it. We have dogs, cats, horses, goats, even a pot-bellied pig. I am a humane investigator for the state, so I see many cases of neglect and abuse. All of our shelter animals come from these kinds of situations. The community has been extremely supportive, and things are going well. P. Pie goes to all the fund-raisers; he's very effective and, of course, extremely photogenic.

I've never had an animal be so loving to me. Sometimes I call him Perfect Pie.

ADDIE AND HUNTER

RUTH AND GEORGE DEHLMAR
Ranchers

Addie was an older dog when she was dropped off at the shelter. How could anyone abandon her? Poor thing, she's the most gentle, sweet dog. I know someone petted her and loved her once. Sometimes it's hard to find homes for older dogs, but just look at Addie. She's quiet, clean and well behaved; there are not many puppies you could describe that way.

Hunter, the beagle, was taken from his owner by the Animal Control officer; the dog had been badly abused. He spent most of his first year here under the bed. Later, he started going off on hunting expeditions. Now he's happy to stay home.

Both dogs are so sweet, so grateful, so appreciative of any kindness. I think most animals who have had a hard time will be that way.

Our daughter has three pound dogs, who sometimes stay at our house. With our dogs, the three cats and our thirty-year-old goose, we're quite a group.

TYLER

JAY WITHERSPOON
Environmental consultant

A friend who volunteers at the SPCA called me one day to say she had found the perfect dog for me and a good companion for my Australian shepherd, Echo. She went on to say the dog is also an Australian shepherd, a beautiful blue merle, a stray picked up in some school yard in San Jose, very sweet and calm, just what Echo needs, and by the way, he is blind. After questioning at some length my friend's definition of perfect, I reluctantly agreed to see the dog. He was sweet and calm, and he handled his blindness remarkably well.

After three more visits, two with Echo and one with a borrowed dog, plus a complete checkup with my vet, Tyler came home with me. He did a complete perimeter check of each room and the backyard (as he always does in a new situation) and settled down to make himself at home. He now races to the door to welcome visitors, avoiding table legs and other obstacles. At home you would never guess he is blind. He and Echo play and wrestle. She has mellowed considerably with his good influence, and he uses her as a guide dog when they run loose in the park. Of course, I keep him on a leash on the street or in any situation that could be dangerous. With me on the other end of the leash, he walks along with confidence. He knows I will alert him to steps and curbs. With someone new he is much more cautious, moving carefully with his nose to the ground.

Tyler is no more burden than a dog with twenty-twenty vision, actually much less than many I have seen. Even now, years later, he gives me a strong sense that he's appreciative and happy to be here with me. My wife, Theresa, and I both find that being with Tyler calms us down. Petting him is relaxing. He's quite cooperative; he would let you pet him all night. I guess my friend was right: Tyler is perfect for me.

JULIET GRAHAM
Horse trainer

ANNIE BISHOP
Student

Juliet: Actually, Henry found me. I was sitting on the porch one evening having a drink with a friend when this big, shaggy, black and white dog walked up the driveway. He had no collar, so when he seemed inclined to hang around, I agreed that he could stay overnight. We named him Henry McKenna because we were drinking Henry McKenna bourbon at the time, and the name seemed to suit him.

Henry did stay overnight. That was nine years ago, and he's still here. I guess it was a lucky day for both of us when he wandered in. He's a grand old man.

Annie: When I was ten, Mom gave me a collar for my birthday and took me to visit the pound. We looked around at lots of dogs, and then I saw Smoky. He was little and so, so cute, about a year old. He seemed very timid and shy, huddled in the back of his cage. Mom thought he was too timid, but I asked the kennel attendant to bring him out for us; and right away we just loved him, and he loved us.

His first owners had taken him to the pound because they said he wasn't housebroken, but he's always been good at our house. They lived in an apartment and took him out about twice a day; he was only a puppy.

He's always with us. He loves my mom, but he definitely knows he's my dog.

BOOMER

DEANNA COLLINS   WAYNE DALTON

We got Boomer from a guy we know. The dog was about a year old and very skinny. He really wasn't doing too well. I don't know what would have happened to him if we hadn't taken him. He's put on some weight since he's been with us, so he looks much better now.

He lives in our tent and hangs out wherever we are. On the street, he's a good retriever. He brings us bottles and cans. He likes to play with them, but, hey, they're worth just as much with a few tooth marks.

We named him Boomer because he always comes back to us, like a boomerang.

HUGO

NANCY HERKIMER

Animal attendant, Hearing Dog Program

Hugo is a hearing dog, a graduate of the San Francisco SPCA Hearing Dog Program, and he works for me. I had spinal meningitis as a baby, so my hearing is impaired. Before I got Hugo, I missed phone calls, people at the door and timer lights that flashed when I wasn't looking at them. Now when the doorbell or the phone rings, Hugo comes to get me. He lets me know when timers go off for cooking and laundry. He jumps up to get my attention and then runs to the door, phone, microwave or whatever made the sound. He also alerts me to the smoke alarm.

Hugo must be a mixture of several breeds. He's long and low with basset legs, a coat and face a little like a spaniel, and a border collie's energy and strong desire to work. But really, who knows? Whatever he is, he's wonderful. He loves to learn things, so I've taught him some tricks. He can balance a treat on his nose, wait patiently for a signal from me, and then flip the treat into the air and catch it. He jumps through a hoop, or through my arms if there's no hoop handy. If I sing Happy Birthday, he joins in, and he also sings while I sign the words.

Because he's a service dog, Hugo can go everywhere with me: stores, restaurants and all public places. He can go on public transportation including planes. He loves planes. He just curls up at my feet and goes to sleep. He's much calmer than I am.

Hugo has made a big difference in my life. You can get special flashing lights to indicate sounds, but Hugo actually comes to find me, and he'll last a lifetime, with no batteries to change.

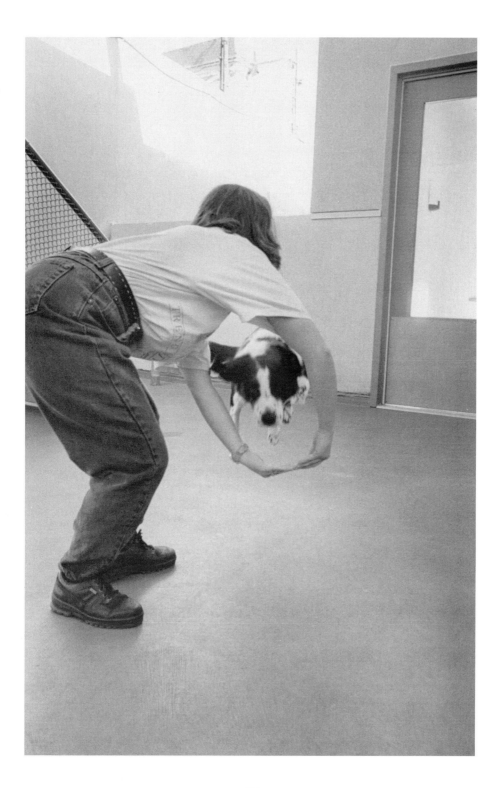

JAKIE

KEVIN O'BRIEN
Real estate developer

When someone asks about Jakie's breed, I tell them he's a dog-pound terrier, and that's exactly what he is. I spent many hours at the shelter helping out and walking dogs; I saw a lot of good dogs, but when Jakie showed up, I knew he had to come home with me. I've never had a bit of trouble with him, except that first day. He ran off and disappeared for three hours; I guess he must have been confused. I waited for a while, hoping he would come back, then drove around the neighborhood calling him and looking for him. When I came home, I noticed that the front door was pushed open, and there was Jakie sitting on the stairs waiting for me. Apparently, he had figured out where home was.

He's the dearest little guy. And talk about devoted; wherever I am, if I look behind me, he's there. His tail never stops wagging, and just look at that face! The only prettier brown eyes I have ever seen belong to my former wife. I've raised many dogs in my life, and Jakie's as good as I've ever seen.

PAL

BOBBY SHORT
Entertainer

Archival photograph

When we were kids, Pal was our adopted dog. He had a lot of German shepherd going for him with a little collie thrown in. He was as great a companion as a dog can be for a kid. I come from a large family, and Pal loved us all, but he adored my mother, and the feeling was mutual.

I learned from Pal what a dog can mean in your life. I have had many dogs since then, and today it's Chili, my Dalmatian, who provides companionship, amusement and a friend who's always happy to see me.

MARLEY AND TEVA-BELLE

SUDIE WOODSON
Interior designer

I have two pound dogs. Marley came first. She's an Airedale mix, very loving with her family, but a little aggressive with other dogs or with strangers coming to the house. People often think that Teva looks scary; little do they know that it's Marley with the sweet whiskery face who's known as The Ripper. You would understand the name if you saw the upholstered chair near the back door, the chair that Marley attacks whenever the garbage man comes to our house. It looks as if ten cats had been sharpening their claws on it for a year. Marley has definite likes and dislikes. She doesn't like cages, so when I go on a trip and the boarding kennel van comes to pick up the dogs, she rides shotgun with the driver. You can see she's good at training people.

After our old dog, Woofer, died, Marley was despondent. I was too, so we adopted Teva. She was a Rottweiler mix, six weeks old, neglected and half-starved. I believe in the sourdough starter theory: You get a puppy while you have an older dog to raise it. Teva was the best puppy even though she does nearly everything Marley the Ripper tells her to do.

The dogs have helped me in my work. Figuring out how to live with them and still have pretty things has been a challenge. I've learned a lot about slipcovers and washable spreads, and, more important, about enjoying a house that looks comfortable and lived in. I like to design interiors that work for people with kids and pets.

The dogs are my companions. They make me laugh and they make me happy. I'd like to say that they are my soulmates, but I'm afraid it might upset my son. He thinks that I am too sentimental about the dogs, and in print it could be especially embarrassing. He says, "Mom, it's not *normal. . . .*"

CHESTER AND SADIE

RENEE NOLAN

JOHN NOLAN
Veterinarians

Renee: At the animal clinic where I worked, we always kept a few shelter dogs and cats to try to find homes for them. Sadie, a black Lab, was with us there for a while. She seemed like a nice dog. She barked a little when people came in, so I thought she might make a good watchdog. Besides, John had always wanted another Lab after his first one died of old age.

One weekend when John was out of town, I decided to bring Sadie home with me to give her a try. Well, I was right about the good watchdog. When John came home I wasn't around, and Sadie refused to let him in the house. We got through that somehow, and I started a campaign to try to bring Sadie and John together.

John: It was, "John, don't you want to feed her? Don't you want to take her for a walk?" Finally, I had to say, "Renee, I'm going to tell you something. I didn't want this dog. I don't even like her. Just give it up."

Renee: But Sadie liked John. She made a huge effort over him, really glommed on to him, and only a few weeks later, he announced, "It's embarrassing to admit this, but I think I'm falling for Sadie."

John: How could I resist?

Renee: Now, about Chester . . . Chester is really my dog.

John: He certainly is. You could say that Chester is pathologically attached to Renee.

Renee: This is the way it happened. I wanted a small, quiet dog. After visiting the shelter two or three times without seeing just the right one, I walked in one day to find that the state had seized twenty-eight dogs from an animal collector, an old woman who was living in a car next to an abandoned house where she kept all these dogs. I walked past Chester's cage three or four times without paying much attention to him. The cage had a sign, Not ready for adoption. Chester looked at me, I looked at him, and it seemed to me he was saying, "It would be really cool if you took me, but I would understand if you didn't." Then he looked away. Did I have a choice?

The shelter personnel had named him Spot because when you took him out of the cage, he stayed in one spot, didn't move. I think he had spent most of his life on a chain.

John: When Renee brought this dog home, I just said, "Why?"

Renee: No question about it, Chester was a mess. It took him weeks to relax. He was scared of everything, scared to walk on a leash, scared to get in the car. He howled whenever I left him, and he trashed the house. I tried behavior modification techniques, even drugs. It all helped a bit, but when Sadie arrived, she helped him more than anything. It was neat to see him gradually get over being so frightened. Why, we hadn't even known his tail could go up.

Sadie and Chester are very close. She's Mariel Hemingway; he's Woody Allen. She's the beautiful, young thing dating this short, older, insecure guy. Chester will probably never be what you might call normal, but he's come a long way, and he's just so sweet, at least to me.

John: Sadie has completely convinced me that the best dog you will ever have is an adopted dog.

LUCY

JESSICA JEWELL
Student

Lucy lived in the city park for months, making nests in the bushes, begging and scrounging for food, until one day, Anita, a friend of my mom's, took the poor dog and started looking for a home for her. Lucy tried two families before us, but Anita didn't think they worked out well enough. We've had her seven or eight years now; I guess we passed the test.

She was always so sweet that I would have been happy to just keep her and cuddle her, but Mom made me sign up for 4-H. We did 4-H for seven years. At first we concentrated on obedience competition, and Lucy was great; she's part Sheltie and very smart. Later we moved on to fitting and showing. Lucy loves it; now that she's older, she would much rather be pretty than work on obedience. This year we were grand champions at the county fair. Lucy is an old pro. Last summer she helped out with a Cloverbud [a younger 4-H member], who was scared of showing and even scared of her own dog. After a few weeks working with Lucy, the girl had all the confidence she needed to train her dog and do really well.

Most of the time Lucy is Miss Priss, very delicate; but when we go out in the woods camping, she rolls in everything, the nastier the better. She digs holes for nests and takes food away to bury it. I think she goes back to her early days as a stray living on her own in the park.

She means a lot to me, even when Mom sends the dogs in to wake me in the morning and Lucy sits on my head. Sometimes I think, What if we had never found her? She's glad we did, and I am too. I love Lucy.

BODIE

ALLEN BLAGDEN
Artist

When I first saw him in the New Mexico desert, Bodie was essentially a wild dog; he looked like many generic dogs I had seen in Central America and Africa. He was brown and very thin, with prick ears and a tail that curved over his back. I returned to the spot where I first saw him several times with picnics, including dog food sandwiches, and although he did seem interested in me and certainly in the sandwiches, he was always wary. Eventually I had to return home to the East Coast, so I left money with neighbors to buy food for the wild dog I couldn't get out of my mind.

A month later, I called to check on the food allowance and learned that Animal Control had picked the dog up, and he had four days left before euthanasia. Frantically, and with no thought for the consequences, I arranged to ransom him with a credit card. Some wonderful friends took him in although he was still very wild and by now thoroughly traumatized. They kept him for several weeks, working on him with the Tellington Touch, and then shipped him to me, heavily tranquilized.

The first few weeks were tough. I kept him on a leash when we were outside, but one day he slipped his collar and ran off. Hours later, when I had just about given up hope, he emerged from under the front porch in time for dinner. I think he knew a good food source when he saw one.

Bodie taught me patience, and little by little rewarded my efforts with his trust. He was very wary at first, but now he sleeps on my bed with all four feet in the air. He came to me at a bad time in my life; I had been recently divorced and had moved out of a house and studio where I had lived and worked for twenty years. I was miserable, but this wild, nervous dog needed me; and seeing him develop a loving, trusting, comical personality has made me happy. I really don't know who saved whom.

SANDY

DON RHINEHART
Manager, remote wilderness lodge

My friend Butch called one day and said, "You've got to see this dog. She's a German wirehaired pointer (Butch's favorite breed). Her name is Sandy. I'll bring her over."

I wasn't so sure. When our old Labrador died, I told my wife, Ginny, "No more dogs! I get to loving them, and then they're gone."

When they arrived, Sandy wouldn't get out of the car. She was a pitiful thing, eight months old, just skin and bones with a ratty-looking coat. She was obviously terrified. She had come from an extremely abusive owner whose wife had persuaded him to turn her over to the shelter when it was obvious that Sandy wasn't going to make a hunting dog, at least not for him. The people at the shelter said that when she first came in she was afraid of everyone. When one of them went to feed her or walk her, she just huddled in the very back of the pen, trembling. They had worked with her for a few weeks, and she was getting a little better with women, but still scared to death of men.

I didn't know what to think, so Butch took Sandy back to the shelter.

Then, a week later, I heard that the shelter was running a picture ad of Sandy in the paper. I called them right away, and when they explained that they couldn't hold dogs, I told them I would be down there in fifteen minutes. I signed her up and brought her home.

When you see a dog like Sandy who has suffered so much, it just makes you sick. I thought maybe I could do something for her; I had to give her a chance.

At first it was tough. She cowered, shook and peed all over herself any time you looked at her. I put a bed for her next to ours and slept with one arm hanging down so she could get used to me. I had to hand-feed her at first; we had quite a time until she began to know she could trust me. It was a long process with a lot of hitches along the way.

Friends who had years of experience with dogs told me there was no way of knowing for sure if Sandy's spirit was broken beyond repair.

Ginny and I manage a wilderness lodge. It is quiet and peaceful there. Sometimes in winter when there is no wind, you can hear a cow elk bark three miles away. I think this place was a big factor in Sandy's recovery. She started to eat; her body filled out and her coat got shiny. She didn't have the nightmares so much anymore. Then she started to show a little silliness, jumping around and clowning a bit. That sure seemed like a good sign. When she began to point squirrels and birds, I figured she might have a chance. Gradually, Sandy began to trust us, and then other people as well. It seemed like a kind of miracle.

I knew I had to get her confidence before I could start any training. I wanted her to know how to be a nice lady, but it was very hard, especially with her background. I had to be so careful not to let her get scared or lose confidence in me. You have to tailor your training to the dog. When you start to lose the dog's attention, whether she's tired or just overloaded, stop the training session, and go take a walk or play. I'm not a real dog trainer, but I did have a book with some good advice:

1. Be firm and consistent.

2. Always remember that if you lose your temper, you are the one with a problem.

3. Take your time, whatever time it takes.

Also, I believe in lots of love and praise. Sandy had to know who was the boss; I think it made her feel more secure. Now, Sandy listens to me. I use a certain whistle to call her. If she was a hundred yards out there with a T-bone steak, she would come when I whistle. It's the most important thing to teach a dog, especially out here in the wilderness where there are packs of coyotes that could kill her and eat her. It wouldn't be the fault of the coyotes; it wouldn't be the dog's fault; it would be mine.

I was raised by my grandfather on a cattle ranch in eastern Washington. All through that first year with Sandy, I often thought of him. He used to say, "Your animals must come first because they can't take care of themselves." Today, Sandy is a fabulous dog, but, you know, you earn that.

Doesn't it just warm your heart to see her now?

BIGFOOT

PAT BEATTIE
Retired riding instructor

My husband used to say, "If I believed in reincarnation, I would like to come back as one of Pat's dogs." Sometimes I wonder about that; you see, Bigfoot has exactly the same big, brown eyes my husband had.

He's a sweet, gentle dog, but then I think adopted dogs are bound to be loving. I should know, I've had a bunch of them. I have never bought a dog because mine have always found me.

BO AND TUXEDO

CAROL SHIVELEY
Director of Education, Oregon Humane Society

Like all puppies, Bo, a golden retriever/Irish setter mix, was adorable when he was young. Unfortunately, his original family couldn't handle the puppy antics, and they gave up on him. The family took him to Animal Control, where he spent two months on a damp concrete floor and developed a malformed hip and a slight limp. Finally a nice couple named Wendy and Mike adopted him, but he proceeded to chase their neighbor's sheep. They reluctantly decided to find another home for him. They placed an ad in the newspaper: Free to a good home. A mother with a little boy answered the ad. They seemed like nice people, so, although Wendy and Mike were sad to see the dog go, Wendy took the phone number of the new owners, and they watched him leave.

A month later, Wendy decided to call to see how Bo was getting on in his new home. She spoke to the woman who had taken him and was disturbed when the woman at first seemed confused about which dog it was and then hurriedly said that he had been hit by a car and killed, *three months before!* This sounded very fishy, so Wendy called both the Oregon Humane Society and the Department of Agriculture, thus providing another clue for what turned out to be an investigation already in progress. Apparently the operator of a kennel licensed to raise animals for sale to laboratories was actually selling pets that had been stolen from backyards or off the street. His preferred method was to have his employees adopt dogs for him. These respectable-looking people, like the mother with a child who took Bo, systematically answered "free to a good home" ads, adopted the animals and brought them to the kennel where they were put in cages to await sale to laboratories for experimental purposes. False documentation on the animals was provided to the labs.

The kennel was raided. The operator was eventually sentenced to eighteen months in federal prison. It was the first successful prosecution under federal law for fraudulently obtaining and selling pets for medical research and animal testing. When he was convicted, the man said, "None of those dogs was worth anything anyway."

The authorities managed to track down some of the dogs who had been sold, at least some of the ones who were still alive. One dog required eight hours of surgery. The vet who had done the repair work adopted her afterward. The dogs from the kennel went to various humane organizations. Bo arrived at the Oregon Humane Society where one look from those big, brown eyes convinced me to take him home.

It took more than big, brown eyes to persuade my husband that this was a good idea. He thought the dog was too big for our house, but Bo soon convinced him otherwise. He folds himself up almost as if he were double-jointed and covers himself with his tail. He manages to go through a tiny dog door. He was clean and relatively easy to housetrain, and he responded well to basic obedience training.

He soon started going to work with me to help in our education program. He and his buddy, Tuxedo, visit schools throughout our area and help present our humane education program. Last year my assistant and I and our dogs met with 22,000 students. Bo knows the routine and loves his job. He works the crowd like a pro, going up and down the rows from desk to desk. Sometimes while I'm giving a presentation he uses a child's foot as a pillow. He provides a good incentive for the students. If they listen to me, Bo will do his tricks for them afterward. He can sit, stay, shake hands (he's ambidextrous) and do a high-five. He rolls over and will get up onto anything I point out.

Bo seems to sense when kids are troubled. One day he spent a great deal of time with one little boy, just sitting quietly while the child petted him. The teacher told me later that the boy's father had recently died. He works wonders with kids who are afraid of dogs. He seems to adjust his response according to each child and each situation. Once, visiting with a little girl in a wheelchair, I gave him the signal to put a paw on her knee. He ignored me and simply put his head gently on her lap. I learned later that the physical therapist had not had the opportunity to tell me that this child's bones were exceptionally fragile.

Bo is certified by the Delta Society in their Pet Partners program. He goes with me to a residential treatment facility for children. They all know him and look forward to his visits. He is very tolerant of these children. He lies down so that the smaller ones can reach him. He adapts to their needs. I could never have taught him this, but he has figured it out for himself.

At home, Bo is the low man in the dog family. Our little poodle mix sometimes chases him into a closet, but Bo did stand up to him once. The little dog can be very crabby and, for some reason, flew at our young grandson one day. Bo intercepted.

I should add that he's not always an angel. He has a real sweet tooth and sometimes steals cookies and even chocolate, which is poisonous to dogs. One day he ate twenty-four gingerbread men, carefully spitting out the red-hot cinnamon eyes and buttons.

Bo sometimes works as a team with his best friend, Tuxedo, our little black and white terrier mix. Just before he was born, Tuxedo's mom was dumped on the side of the road and then rescued by a passerby who brought her to the Humane Society. She produced only one puppy, Tuxedo. I adopted him when he was eight weeks old. Tuxedo and Bo have always been close. They remind me of Arnold Schwarzenegger and Danny Devito in the movie *Twins*. One large, one small, both the same age and both males, they are an odd pair, but they are buddies. Sometimes Tuxedo kisses Bo until the big dog finally puts a paw on the little one's head to hold him at bay.

Tuxedo is a comical little dog. When he sits up, he looks like a penguin; and when he rolls his eyes, he looks like one of those Felix the Cat clocks. Sometimes he wears a bow tie on the job. He is involved in animal-assisted therapy and the Delta Society's Pet Partners. He visits rest homes, hospitals and rehabilitation centers. He especially loves kids. He will kiss them if they touch the end of his nose. Like Bo, he is very intuitive. Several psychiatrists have used him for treating phobias. Tuxedo works well with troubled kids. Whether they are acting out or seriously depressed, he will sit with them and comfort them. Since he is so little and so funny-looking, he is not threatening.

One day I was asked to bring Tuxedo into an intensive care unit where a young girl was showing almost no sign of life. When I held Tuxedo near the bed, her vital signs began to improve. The hospital staff requested more visits because the patient showed some interest in the dog and in nothing else. When we moved him around the room, she followed him with her eyes. Otherwise, she seemed almost catatonic. Another time we were asked to visit a boy who was in a coma. Tuxedo licked his face. The child opened his eyes and said, "Nice, warm puppy."

Both Bo and Tuxedo are special, but then I believe that all dogs are special. They just need love to bring it out.

ADOPTING A DOG

If you are thinking of adopting a dog, there are several important steps that can help make this important endeavor successful, both for you and for the dog you choose. Jon Kellar (p. 4) and Alison Lufkin (p. 74) describe the process each went through.

1. Define for yourself, as specifically as you can, exactly what you are looking for in a dog. Is it companionship, and if so, what sort of companionship? Are you thinking about long walks, sitting together on the sofa, company in the office, strenuous hikes in the mountains, about all of the above or none of the above? Would you like a dog to work with, perhaps in agility trials, obedience competition or search and rescue? How do you see a dog sharing your life?

2. Be as realistic as possible about how a dog will actually fit into your life. How much time do you have to devote to care, exercise, grooming and training? Do you travel? What will you do about vacations? A dog is a social creature, a pack animal, and needs companionship. He or she is not a stuffed animal to snuggle with when you are in the mood and to ignore the rest of the time. A dog who doesn't get enough attention will be an unhappy dog and probably a nuisance as well. If you work all day and have classes, meetings or social events in the evenings, you might want to consider adopting a cat instead. Some cats are quite content to have the house to themselves during a major part of the day as long as they are fed well and given attention at a time of their choice.

3. If you are looking for a dog to be a companion and playmate for a dog you already own, consider carefully how this will work. Often a dog with too much energy is not getting enough attention from his owner; adding another dog to the family can make this situation worse. Never bring two new dogs or puppies into your life at the same time. They will bond to one another, and you will be peripheral at best.

4. Learn about different breeds and what you can expect from them. This knowledge can be helpful in evaluating mixed breeds as well as purebreds. Talk to dog owners, trainers, vets and shelter personnel. Educate yourself. Read. There are several helpful books specifically about adopting dogs, and many training books discuss the process of choosing a dog. (See Recommended Reading.) Try not to be seduced simply on the basis of looks. Focus on breeds or mixtures of breeds that best fit your personality and lifestyle. Consider temperament, activity and size, as well as what the particular breed is designed to do.

Hunting dogs may retrieve anything that is not nailed down, and they are apt to roam if unsupervised. Some herding dogs have such an intense desire to work that they need a job or at least an owner who is prepared to spend time training them and giving them an occupation, whether it be herding or agility trials. Otherwise, these dogs may find a job for themselves, and it may involve chasing cars.

Be aware that some breeds have a predisposition to medical problems such as hip dysplasia, deafness, seizures or various forms of cancer.

5. Consider the expense involved. Shelter personnel or a veterinarian can help you anticipate, at least in a general way, the costs of owning a dog. A good-quality food is important, and there will always be medical bills. Even a young, healthy dog needs immunizations and may have an accident or injury.

Once you have evaluated your situation, decided that you *do* want to look for a dog, and have a sense of what kind of a dog you would like, what next? Some veterinarians place homeless animals. Shelters, sadly, are usually full of them. Wherever you go, bear in mind several points.

1. Talk with the people caring for the animals. Explain what you are looking for. Ask about the dog's history and temperament. If you sense that they are not interested or are trying to talk you into taking an animal simply because he or she needs a home ("If you don't adopt him, he's going to be euthanized tomorrow!"), go somewhere else. Responsible people in the business of placing animals understand the importance of making a good match. After all, they are the ones who see every day the sad results of decisions made on impulses like "What a cute puppy! Wouldn't it be fun to have one!"

2. If you are interested in a specific breed, inquire at shelters. Purebred dogs do turn up there. Most breed clubs have rescue and re-homing groups that place dogs of that breed. Call the parent club of the breed in which you are interested. On the Internet, Dog Forum lists breed rescue and re-homing groups.

3. Consider an adult dog. Some may have problems relating to their previous experiences or lack thereof, but in most cases, with some thoughtful attention and training, such problems can be resolved. With an adult dog you may get a better sense of how he or she will turn out, allowing, of course, for temporary depression or overexcitement caused by stress. A puppy can be a surprise package.

4. Do not bring children, especially young ones, with you to help choose a dog. It is a sure route to an impulse choice that you may regret later. Wait until you have a good idea of the dog you want, and then bring the children along to see how the dog and the children interact.

5. Do not take a dog simply because you feel sorry for the poor thing. With any luck the dog you adopt will be with you for ten or fifteen years, perhaps longer, and it is just as important for the dog's sake as it is for yours that the relationship be a happy and successful one.

6. Visit the dog several times before making a decision. Take him or her for walks if possible. Notice how the dog responds to other dogs and to people, including you.

7. If you feel at all unsure, go to other shelters and look at other dogs.

8. Bring family members and possibly other pets to meet a dog that you are seriously considering. This is an exception to #4 above. In this case you are bringing children to meet a specific dog, not presenting them with the option of any dog at the shelter.

9. Take your time. This is an important decision and a major commitment. Talk it over with people whom you respect, especially people who have had experience with dogs. Think about it. Sleep on it.

If, after all this, you decide to go ahead and adopt the dog that you have been considering, it is a good idea to do some planning before you bring your new pet home.

1. Make an appointment for a veterinary checkup for your new dog as soon as possible. Plan to bring records of any known immunizations, as well as a stool sample. You may also want to schedule an appointment with a groomer.

2. Lay in some supplies such as a bed, bowls for food and water, and enough dog food for a few days. If you use the same food that the dog has been eating, he or she will be less prone to upset stomach problems during the excitement of adjusting to a new life. You may want to discuss a quality dog food with your vet when the dog has an initial exam. Good pet stores can provide advice on food. You may want to purchase a few toys, including something appealing and safe to chew, but don't go overboard. After you have spent some time with your dog, you will have a much better sense of his or her preferences. A crate or airline kennel is an invaluable tool for easing a dog into a new environment. Your dog will soon regard the crate as a den or refuge, especially if it is not overused.

3. Dog-proof your home as much as possible, removing potentially dangerous objects as well as things that could be damaged. Designate an area where the dog can comfortably spend time with you. Do not give a new dog the run of the house.

4. Decide with your family or roommates what the rules are to be so that from the start you can teach right from wrong. Consistency is extremely important.

Finally the big day arrives. You fill out the adoption forms, pay the fees, and take the dog home with you. It is an exciting experience, the beginning of a new relationship. Remember, it is only the beginning.

1. When you first bring the dog home, try to keep the atmosphere relatively calm and quiet.

Introduce family members and pets in a controlled way. Never leave a new dog unsupervised with children or with other pets until you have a good sense of his or her potential reaction, not to mention the potential reaction of the child or pet in residence. Children must be supervised and trained to be gentle with animals, for their own sake as well as the animals'.

2. Use the crate or kennel. Most dogs naturally like a place of their own—a den—and a crate can serve this purpose. Feeding the dog in the crate can help to make this den more appealing. Crating a dog when it is to be alone will avoid undesirable behavior, such as chewing or soiling. Of course, you should not leave a dog for long hours in a crate. Use common sense.

3. Spend as much time as you possibly can with your dog. This is especially important in the beginning. Plan to bring your dog home over a weekend or, better still, during a vacation. During this time occasionally leave the dog alone for short periods, preferably in the crate. He or she needs to learn that your departure does not mean abandonment.

4. Be patient. Remember that your dog has been through some stressful, perhaps even traumatic, experiences. He or she needs time to settle down and to learn what you expect. Set your dog up to succeed. Try to anticipate the dog's actions in order to avoid letting him or her make mistakes. As much as possible, orchestrate situations so that you can say "Good dog!" rather than "Bad dog!" Be sure to compliment and reward good behavior frequently. Use a positive approach; your dog will learn easily and quickly.

5. Exercise is important. Both you and the dog will feel better, and the dog will probably behave better as well. Who knows, maybe you will too! Do check with your vet on the appropriate level of exercise. You can overdo it, especially with puppies, older dogs, dogs with physical problems or dogs who have been leading a relatively sedentary life. Start out slowly, use common sense and take your cues from the dog. Remember that most dogs are eager to please and may overtire without complaining.

6. Enroll the dog in an obedience class. You may want to arrange for a private consultation with a trainer to evaluate the dog and to learn how best to work with him or her. Such a consultation may seem expensive, but it can be a valuable investment in the long run.

Research carefully before choosing a trainer for consultation or for classes. Ask friends who have had successful experiences with obedience classes. If possible, attend a class as an observer. A trainer can be a valuable ally in your efforts to include your new dog in your life. You should be comfortable with the training methods and the way the trainer treats students, both human and canine. A trainer who kicks or hits a dog or suspends one by the collar is probably a trainer to avoid. You should not, however, be put off by a trainer who administers a strong physical correction to a dog who is aggressive to a person or to another dog. A good trainer will understand the importance of tailoring all training to the individual. Methods that might be effective with a dominant, strong-minded dog would probably not be appropriate for a more submissive, timid dog. Your job is to learn to understand your individual dog.

There are many good books on dog training. (See Recommended Reading.) They are probably most effective when used in conjunction with actual classes.

A well-behaved, socialized dog can be included in all aspects of your life. Such a dog can visit friends with you, travel with you in the car, share vacations and perhaps even accompany you to work.

Heed the advice of the Monks of New Skete in *The Art of Raising a Puppy*: "In our view, the dog is not a possession, a personal commodity to be used solely for our own amusement or ego gratification. Rather, it is a living, autonomous, yet highly social, pack-oriented creature that has an amazing capacity for companionship and love. Your role in determining whether this will be the case for your own dog is a vital one. Capacity is precisely that, a natural potential. A good relationship with your dog can be established only if there is an enlightened commitment to working with its proven needs, instincts, behaviour patterns, and, yes, capacities."

Work with your dog, include your dog in your life and, most important, enjoy your dog!

ORGANIZATIONS

ADOPTION

Local animal shelters are listed in your phone book.

Most breed clubs have rescue and re-homing groups.

The Internet lists various breed-rescue organizations. Many humane organizations have World Wide Web pages to provide information on animals available for adoption.

Veterinarians sometimes place homeless animals. Speak to your vet and ask for referrals.

Pets Are Wonderful Support (PAWS) is a volunteer organization in San Francisco that helps people with AIDS keep their animal companions. At times, PAWS needs to find homes for animals whose owners have passed away. For more information, call (415) 241-1460.

Greyhound Pets of America places former racing greyhounds. For more information call 1-800-366-1472.

ACTIVITIES TO SHARE
Agility

United States Dog Agility Association
P.O. Box 850955
Richardson, TX 75085-0955

The American Kennel Club
51 Madison Avenue, New York, NY 10010
(212) 696-8800
The AKC can provide information on clubs involved in many different activities, such as agility, obedience, herding, tracking, carting and sled pulling.

Obedience Competition

The American Mixed Breed Obedience Registration (also agility and other activities)
205 1st Street SW
New Prague, MN 56071
(612) 758-4598

Pet-Assisted Therapy

The Delta Society
Pet Partners Program
289 Perimeter Road East
Renton, WA 98055-1329
(206) 226-7357
E-mail: deltasociety@cis.compuserve.com

Search and Rescue

The American Rescue Dog Association (ARDA)
P.O. Box 151
Chester, NY 10918

Terrier Field Trials

The American Working Terrier Association
Gordon Heldebrant
2406 Watson Street
Sacramento, CA 95864
(916) 485-5950

Don't forget walking, hiking, backpacking, and camping—all activities that are fun to share with a dog.

RECOMMENDED READING

ADOPTION

Benjamin, Carol Lea. *Second Hand Dog*. New York: Howell Book House, 1988.

Branigan, Cynthia A. *Adopting the Racing Greyhound*. New York: Howell Book House, 1993.

Kilcommons, Brian, and Michael Capuzzo. *Mutts, America's Dogs: A Guide to Choosing, Loving and Living with our Most Popular Canine*. New York: Warner Books, 1996.

Rubenstein, Eliza, and Shari Kalina. *The Adoption Option: Choosing, Training, and Raising the Shelter Dog for You*. New York: Howell Book House, 1996.

TRAINING

Benjamin, Carol Lea. *Mother Knows Best*. New York: Howell Book House, 1985.

Kilcommons, Brian, with Sarah Wilson. *Good Owners, Great Dogs*. New York: Warner Books, 1992.

The Monks of New Skete. *The Art of Raising a Puppy*. Boston: Little, Brown and Company, 1991.

The Monks of New Skete. *How to Be Your Dog's Best Friend, A Training Manual for Dog Owners*. Boston: Little, Brown and Company, 1978.

Myer, Nicki. *A Pet Owner's Guide to the Dog Crate*. Weston, CT: Educational Effort Inc. To order, call (203) 226-9877.

Rutherford, Clarice and David H. Neil. *How to Raise a Puppy You Can Live With*. Loveland, CO: Alpine Publishing, 1992.